... and the Pursuit of Happiness

... and the Pursuit of Happiness

Wellbeing and the Role of Government

EDITED BY PHILIP BOOTH

The Institute of Economic Affairs

First published in Great Britain in 2012 by
The Institute of Economic Affairs
2 Lord North Street
Westminster
London sw1p 3lb
in association with Profile Books Ltd

The mission of the Institute of Economic Affairs is to improve public understanding of the fundamental institutions of a free society, with particular reference to the role of markets in solving economic and social problems.

A CIP catalogue record for this book is available from the British Library.

ISBN 978 0 255 36656 4

Many IEA publications are translated into languages other than English or are reprinted. Permission to translate or to reprint should be sought from the Director General at the address above.

Typeset in Stone by MacGuru Ltd
info@macguru.org.uk

Printed and bound in Britain by Hobbs the Printers

CONTENTS

PART TWO: HAPPINESS AND GOVERNMENT INTERVENTION

PART THREE: MADE HAPPY BY GOVERNMENT OR FREE TO PURSUE HAPPINESS?

ABOUT THE AUTHORS

Christian Bjørnskov

Christian Bjørnskov is associate professor of economics at Aarhus University in Denmark. He studied economics at Aarhus and obtained a PhD at the Aarhus School of Business in 2005. His research interests include political economy, institutional economics and happiness studies. Christian is on the editorial board of *Public Choice* and the *European Journal of Political Economy* and is affiliated with the Centre for Political Studies in Copenhagen. His research has appeared in a wide range of journals, such as the *Journal of Development Economics*, the *Journal of Law and Economics*, *Public Choice* and the *Journal of Happiness Studies*. More details are available at http://pure.au.dk/portal/da/chbj@asb.dk.

Peter Boettke

Peter Boettke is a university professor of economics at George Mason University (GMU) and the BB&T Professor for the Study of Capitalism at the Mercatus Center at GMU. He is also the editor-in-chief of the *Review of Austrian Economics*. Pete's personal web page is http://econfaculty.gmu.edu/pboettke/.

Philip Booth

Philip Booth is Editorial and Programme Director of the Institute of Economic Affairs and Professor of Insurance and Risk Management at Cass Business School, City University. He has written extensively on regulation, social insurance and Catholic social teaching. He is a Fellow of the Institute of Actuaries and of the Royal Statistical Society and associate editor of *Actuarial Annals* and the *British Actuarial Journal*. He has also advised the Bank of England on financial stability issues (1998–2002) and has been a visiting Fellow at Blackfriars Hall, Oxford University (2010/11).

Christopher Coyne

Christopher Coyne is the F. A. Harper Professor of Economics at the Mercatus Center at George Mason University. He is also the North American editor of the *Review of Austrian Economics*. Chris's personal web page is www.ccoyne.com.

Marc De Vos

Marc De Vos is a professor at the Ghent University law school and the general director of the Itinera Institute, a non-partisan policy think tank based in Brussels. He frequently publishes, lectures and debates on issues of European integration, globalisation, labour market reform, pensions, ageing, healthcare and the welfare state. He has authored and co-authored numerous books and articles. His most recent book is *After the Meltdown: The Future of Capitalism and Globalization in the Age of the Twin Crises* (Shoehorn, 2010).

Paul Ormerod

Paul Ormerod is the author of three best-selling books on economics: *The Death of Economics, Butterfly Economics* and *Why Most Things Fail*, a *Business Week* US Business Book of the Year. He read economics at Cambridge and obtained an MPhil in economics at Oxford, and in 2009 was awarded a DSc *honoris causa* by the University of Durham for the 'distinction of his contributions to economics'. Paul is a consultant but retains close academic links and publishes in a wide range of journals, such as *Proceedings of the Royal Society (Biology), Physica A, Mind and Society* and the *Journal of Economic Interaction and Co-ordination*. More details are available at www.paulormerod.com.

Daniel Sacks

Daniel Sacks is a doctoral student in the Applied Economics Program at the Wharton School of the University of Pennsylvania. His research is supported by a National Science Foundation Graduate Research Fellowship.

Pedro Schwartz

Pedro Schwartz is Professor Extraordinary of Economics at San Pablo University in Madrid. His knowledge of utilitarianism and happiness economics comes from work for a PhD thesis on *The New Political Economy of John Stuart Mill* at the LSE, as well as his time at the Bentham Project. He writes on questions of political philosophy from an economic point of view and is preparing an English translation of his book *In Search of Montesquieu*. For the IEA he wrote *The Euro as Politics* (2004).

J. R. Shackleton

J. R. Shackleton is Professor of Economics at the University of Buckingham and an IEA Fellow. He was previously Dean of the Business Schools at the Universities of East London and Westminster. He has also taught at Queen Mary, University of London, and been an economic adviser in the Government Economic Service. His research interests focus primarily on labour markets and employment issues. He has published widely in both academic and popular media and has appeared many times on radio and TV.

Christopher Snowdon

Christopher Snowdon read history at Lancaster University and has been a full-time author and journalist since 2009. His research focuses on prohibition, junk science and public health. He is the author of *The Spirit Level Delusion* and *Velvet Glove, Iron Fist: A History of Anti-Smoking*. His most recent book is *The Art of Suppression: Pleasure, Panic and Prohibition since 1800.*

Betsey Stevenson

Betsey Stevenson is an assistant professor of business and public policy at Wharton University of Pennsylvania. She received her Masters and PhD in economics from Harvard University in 1999 and 2001, respectively. Betsey is the visiting assistant professor and visiting associate research scholar in the Industrial Relations Section of the Department of Economics at Princeton University. She is affiliated with the National Bureau of Economic Research, the American Law and Economics Association, and CESifo in

Munich. She has published many articles that have appeared in journals such as *Contemporary Economic Policy*, the *Quarterly Journal of Economics* and the *Journal of Labor Economics*.

Justin Wolfers

Justin Wolfers is an associate professor of business and public policy at Wharton University of Pennsylvania. He attended Harvard University from 1997 to 2001 and has a PhD and an AM in economics. Justin's research interests include law and economics, labour economics, social policy, political economy, behavioural economics and macroeconomics. He is a research associate for the National Bureau for Economic Research and is currently affiliated with the Center for the Study of Poverty and Inequality, Kiel Institute for the World Economy and the Brookings Institution. Justin has published articles in journals such as *Contemporary Economic Policy*, the *Quarterly Journal of Economics* and the *American Economic Journal: Economic Policy*. He has also published research for the World Bank.

FOREWORD

'I am not sure whether what you've just argued for is trivial or wrong, but I am certain it's one or the other': so said my tutor at my first moral philosophy tutorial as an undergraduate.

I had just finished reading out my essay – an impassioned defence of the theory of utilitarianism.

Utilitarianism seemed to me, at first glance, to be incontrovertible. The right course of action to take was the one that maximised the greatest happiness of the greatest number. All other considerations needed to be subordinate to this 'greatest felicity principle', as Jeremy Bentham, the most influential contributor to utilitarian theory, termed it.

Even to a (not very well-read) freshman, there were some obvious problems with utilitarian ethics – contestability about how to measure happiness being just one of the more minor irritations. Should we be concerned with the aggregate total of human happiness or should distributional factors be considered? Might the average, rather than aggregate, happiness of human beings be a more desirable aim? How should inter-generational concerns be accounted for – would it be legitimate to alter the happiness of today's population at the expense, or to the benefit, of the unborn? Do only humans count – or do all sentient beings need to be factored in to our overarching happiness-maximising equation?

For a few days at least, however, these seemed to be mere nuances of possible disagreement within a highly attractive universal ethical theory. If human happiness was not to be the key guide to our decision-making, what would?

Fortunately, not many weeks passed before I was introduced to the work of John Rawls and Robert Nozick, who both contributed to clarifying the morally counter-intuitive nature of utilitarianism and establishing a more liberal, individualistic framework for political theory.

Nozick's discussion of an experience machine is perhaps the most keenly analysed and contested section of his work. In short, he asks us to consider the hypothetical opportunity of plugging ourselves into some form of device which would generate the sensations of a life happier than the one we would otherwise lead. We would experience greater levels of ecstasy and fewer feelings of pain if we would just strap ourselves into this 'orgasmatron' and flick on the switch.

Not only would we recoil at actually forcing our fellow citizens into such machines, we would also choose not to take up the entirely voluntary option ourselves. We would, without hesitation, plump for the less happy but more individualistic path. We would most likely consider anyone deciding to enter the machine themselves as committing some form of suicide. Happiness is not something we simply want to experience; it's something we want to achieve.

But if utilitarianism has been tackled successfully in the sphere of moral philosophy, it threatens to make a re-emergence in the field of economics.

'Wellbeing' or 'happiness' economics purports to show that traditional measures of economic 'success' – such as gross domestic product – are simply aiming at the wrong target. Some suggest that, when you ask people how satisfied they are with various aspects of their lives, there is little correlation with material wealth. The way to increase happiness, they claim their research shows, is to strive for a more equal division of resources and a larger role for the state. We should therefore be seeking to maximise people's happiness responses in opinion poll surveys rather than the number of pounds, dollars or euros in their pockets.

This monograph brings together a series of essays which do two things. Those essays that mainly fall in the second half of the monograph examine the fundamental premise that the government should try to maximise wellbeing as the prime minister has implied – this relates to the philosophical issues that I wrestled with as an undergraduate. What happens when this approach conflicts with fundamental moral precepts or inhibits liberty to an unacceptable degree? If government intervention to increase national income does not work, then why should government intervention to increase measured wellbeing? Should we direct society towards a single common goal?

The earlier essays examine some common empirical myths that are often used to justify government intervention to promote wellbeing. In summary, they show that unequal societies are not, in fact, less happy and how wellbeing indicators are very blunt measures that are not generally related to other variables to which we would expect them to be related. One chapter also takes on the so-called Easterlin paradox and shows that happiness is related to income and economic growth – there is no conflict between GDP and GWB (general wellbeing), as the prime minister has suggested there is.

All in all, these essays, by some of the world's leading authors in this field, challenge both the arguments and the conclusions of those 'happiness economists' who believe in deliberate government action and planning to increase measured wellbeing. They demonstrate that, in the main, the case they make is either trivial or wrong.

The views expressed in this monograph are, as in all IEA publications, those of the authors and not those of the Institute (which has no corporate view), its managing trustees, Academic Advisory Council Members or senior staff.

MARK LITTLEWOOD

Director General and Ralph Harris Fellow,
Institute of Economic Affairs

December 2011

SUMMARY

- The idea put forward by the British government that economists and politicians pursue policies directed towards maximising GDP is a 'straw man'. Government has always had a multitude of different objectives and government policy would be very different today if economic growth were the single priority.

- Explicit attempts by government to control GDP, or rapidly increase GDP growth, have normally failed. Such a target-driven mentality is part of the conceit of central planning. Attempts to centrally direct policy towards improving general wellbeing will also fail.

- Contrary to popular perception, new statistical work suggests that happiness is related to income. This relationship holds between countries, within countries and over time. The relationship is robust and also holds at higher levels of income as well as at lower levels of income. This calls into question the assertion that people are on a 'hedonic treadmill' that prevents them becoming happier as their income rises beyond a certain level of income.

- This new work, using a data set of 126 countries, shows that the correlation between life satisfaction and the log of permanent income within a given country lies between 0.3 and 0.5. There is a similar correlation between growth in life satisfaction and growth in income.

- There is no evidence that equality is related to happiness. Indeed, the proponents of greater income equality admit that they are unable to cite such evidence and instead rely on very unsatisfactory forms of indirect inference. The clearest determinants of wellbeing would seem to be employment, marriage, religious belief and avoiding poverty. None of these is obviously correlated with income equality.

- The government is under pressure to bring in further legislation to promote 'wellbeing at work'. This includes, for example, legislation on parental leave. The theoretical and empirical case for such legislation is weak. There is no relationship between objective measures of wellbeing at work and the extent of employment protection legislation, unionisation, and so on. Given the relationship between wellbeing and employment, any form of employment protection legislation that led to more temporary employment or reduced employment would be detrimental to wellbeing.

- A comparison across 74 countries finds that government final consumption negatively affects happiness levels and that the negative influence occurs regardless of how effective government bureaucracy is or how democratic the country is. Increasing government spending by about a third would cause a direct reduction in happiness of about 5 to 6 per cent. Centralising government decision-making is likely to lead to more intrusive government and lower wellbeing.

- If people wish to maximise their wellbeing and are the best judges of their own wellbeing they will take decisions about how to use their economic resources to pursue their own goals. We should allow people's preferences for wellbeing to be revealed by their own actions rather than through surveys of what people say they prefer.

- Happiness measures are short-term, transient and shallow measures of people's genuine wellbeing.
- Those who wish to use happiness economics in public policy have no effective way of determining whether an increase in wellbeing should be traded against justice, moral values or a decrease in freedom. It is a utilitarian philosophy which applies a principle that many might use in their own lives to the organisation of society as a whole. Applying such an overarching principle to the organisation of society as a whole is very dangerous.

FIGURES AND TABLES

... and the Pursuit of Happiness

1 INTRODUCTION
Philip Booth

Politicians in a muddle

Nearly six years ago, David Cameron made a speech in which he suggested: 'It's time we admitted that there's more to life than money, and it's time we focused not just on GDP, but on GWB – general well-being.'[1] The IEA responded with a monograph written by Helen Johns and the author of one of the chapters in this collection, Paul Ormerod. In a later speech David Cameron sounded more sceptical of the wellbeing (or happiness[2]) agenda and actually referred to the Johns and Ormerod publication in the speech. Twelve months ago, however, David Cameron decided to enter the fray again stating: '[measures of wellbeing] could give us a general picture of whether life is improving' and eventually 'lead to government policy that is more focused not just on the bottom line, but on all those things that make life worthwhile'.[3] In doing

---

1   The 2006 speech to Google Zeitgeist can be found at: http://www.guardian.co.uk/politics/2006/may/22/conservatives.davidcameron.

2   The two concepts are used more or less interchangeably throughout this monograph, though there is some discussion of different aspects of happiness or wellbeing in various chapters.

3   The 2010 speech can be found at: http://www.number10.gov.uk/news/pm-speech-on-well-being/. This speech was also notable for three examples of the broken-window fallacy used to justify the measurement of wellbeing rather than national income. The prime minister actually suggested that crime, disease and an earthquake could increase GDP because they increased spending

so, he announced a major government spending project to find out how to measure happiness and wellbeing.

So we are now back where we were in 2006 with the same contradictions, paradoxes and dilemmas. The now prime minister said in 2006: 'Well-being can't be measured by money or traded in markets. It can't be required by law or delivered by government,' and then, within seconds, he suggested that: 'Improving our society's sense of well-being is, I believe, the central political challenge of our times ... I believe that a new political agenda with well-being, as well as wealth creation, as its aim must find ways to address these challenges.' Can the government deliver wellbeing or can't it?

A few moments later in the same speech, the issue became no clearer:

> There are some on the right who might say that this has got nothing to do with politics – that we should leave it all to the market and not interfere ... But what kind of politics is it that has nothing to say about such a central aspect of people's lives? ... [W]e have to show that politics can make a positive difference ... The traditional response of the right – that government can't do much about all this and shouldn't try – is inadequate. But equally, the response of the new left – that government should regulate the specific details of working life – is ineffective. It produces unintended consequences.

He went on to say that the new approach would involve education, exhortation and leadership.

There are good reasons why the speech that defines the

---

on locks, new buildings and so on! This was not even suggested as a short-run phenomenon.

current government's approach to this issue was full of contra-dictions – it is a genuinely complex issue from the perspective of both positive economics and philosophy. Complex issues need careful consideration that avoids woolly thinking. The papers in this monograph help substantially to resolve these issues and also help provide empirical evidence on the policies that should be avoided if the government is to promote wellbeing. Indeed, the papers in the second half of the volume broadly suggest that the government should not be consciously promoting wellbeing but, rather, ensuring that the conditions exist in which people can find happiness themselves.

GDP or GWB?

The papers at the beginning of this volume deal with a number of myths. Paul Ormerod accepts that it is difficult to find a rela-tionship between income and happiness – and that there are a number of good reasons for this. Many people – including in government – use this conclusion to suggest that the government should pursue other goals instead. Indeed, the prime minister used this explicit justification for the pursuit of 'GWB' in his 2010 speech – he suggested that happiness has flatlined as income has increased. The following chapter in this monograph takes this issue on directly and puts forward important evidence that contra-dicts the prime minister's assertion. But, notwithstanding this, Ormerod shows that it is difficult, in fact, to find a relationship between happiness and most other variables (equality, govern-ment spending, and so on ...). Thus, it would seem, politicians have no basis in evidence at all for any public policy based on the pursuit of general wellbeing. There are good reasons for this, including the fact that measured happiness is a bounded measure whereas national income is not. In other words, the difficulty of finding these relationships between income and happiness arises from complex statistical properties of the data.

Furthermore, Ormerod argues that it is impossible to predict and control wellbeing and, indeed, politicians have been too confident in the past about their ability to predict and control GDP. The pursuit of general wellbeing would be the ultimate manifestation of the target-driven mentality that has undermined confidence in government.

Ormerod makes another important point. It is simply a myth that government tries to maximise national income as the prime minister suggests. The prime minister, when he makes that assertion, is simply putting up a straw man to justify a collectivist position. It is also worth noting that he is using the same tactic when he states: 'there are some on the right who might say that this [wellbeing] has got nothing to do with politics – that we should leave it all to the market'. Nobody on the right – if, by that pejorative term, the prime minister means those who believe in a free economy – takes this position. Those who believe in a free economy are acutely aware of the importance of that part of the free economy which exists outside the market and that part of life more generally which is not subject to direct economic considerations. This does not mean, however, that they believe that these aspects of our lives should be within the scope of government control.

Though Ormerod is sceptical about the ability of the wellbeing data to tell us very much, Sacks, Stevenson and Wolfers have undertaken important new empirical research that looks at – and challenges – the Easterlin paradox which lies at the heart of the more interventionist aspects of the wellbeing agenda. The

Easterlin paradox suggests that, as income rises beyond a certain level, wellbeing stagnates – or, at least, that there is no evidence of wellbeing increasing with income. Some use this to promote egalitarian policies on the ground that this will raise happiness whereas a general increase in income cannot. The authors of this chapter, however, note that the mere fact that economists have, hitherto, found little evidence of happiness increasing with income does not mean that happiness does not increase with income – it could also mean that the evidence has not yet been found. The absence of evidence of a relationship between wellbeing and income is not evidence of the absence of such a relationship. Indeed, Sacks and his co-authors find substantial evidence that happiness is higher in countries with higher average income; that it is higher among higher-income individuals; and that, within a country, happiness grows over time as income grows. These findings are robust and use an extremely rich set of data.

Many commentators who suggest that income and happiness are unrelated imply that there is evidence to demonstrate that greater equality will bring greater happiness and put forward hypotheses to back up their claims. Snowdon's chapter deals with this, among other issues. His conclusion speaks for itself:

> In summary, there is no credible evidence that people in more egalitarian countries enjoy happier lives, nor is there any empirical reason to think they should. Scholars of happiness have identified many factors which improve life satisfaction scores but income equality is not one of them. Furthermore, none of the factors which *have* been shown to boost happiness are more prevalent in the "more equal" nations so it is unlikely that those societies would be happier even by chance.

Happiness and government intervention

The first three chapters taken together would suggest that the evidence leads strongly in a direction contrary to the one that the government wishes to take – though, as has been noted above, the government's own position on this subject is not without its internal contradictions. The next section of the monograph tackles the issue of government intervention head on. If the happiness agenda is going to lead the government to intervene in economic and social life to a greater extent then, just as with interventions to try to increase national income, it is reasonable to assume that there will be unforeseen consequences.

This point is made by Bjørnskov, who uses the public choice literature. Centrally planning our wellbeing will be every bit as difficult as centrally planning our economy. Even if the government argues that it does not want to regulate directly but rather to cajole and educate, as David Cameron suggests, how do we know that the government will cajole and educate in the right direction, or will there be unforeseen consequences here too? Bjørnskov finds that there is ample evidence of an inverse relationship between government intervention and wellbeing. We should not compare the outcome of a free economy with the theoretical outcome of government intervention in which it is assumed that the government is run by omniscient angels.

Shackleton looks at a particular aspect of regulation – the labour market. There is a huge literature on wellbeing at work, much of which suggests that government intervention can improve wellbeing. Shackleton warns that different factors are important for different people in bringing about wellbeing at work and that employers have an incentive to respond to the preferences of their workforce (in crude terms a given worker could be paid less if other aspects of the job made him happier). If employment regulation were to limit the variety of jobs that were available, this would be damaging for wellbeing and, if such regulation were to raise unemployment, it would be catastrophic for wellbeing! This chapter by Shackleton demonstrates what is true in so many fields – self-organising persons take decisions that improve their wellbeing: acting both individually and collectively but freely and without the intervention of government.

Made happy by government or free to pursue happiness?

This observation leads on to the third section of the monograph. This is made up of chapters that examine whether the government should be promoting our happiness, maximising our happiness or whether it should focus on creating the framework in which persons can pursue happiness. For different reasons, the authors of these chapters come to that last conclusion. Vos covers some more general issues – also discussed elsewhere in the book – but his analysis brings in some important new points. He questions the whole notion of whether we should be trying to create 'Happyland'. Human achievements are often born out of great adversity. Overcoming great challenges may not cause an increase in transient measured happiness but may lead somebody to be deeply satisfied with their life at a much later time. We should not deliberately try to create adversity and grim living conditions, of course, but we should not try to limit adversity simply to make us happier. Vos then moves on to look at a fundamental trade-off. We may well have to decide whether we promote happiness or justice. And happiness economics has little to say about morality as the basis for individual decision-making. It is, in the words of Vos, 'unbearably light' as a concept. If undermining property rights increases happiness and maximising happiness is the standard by which we judge the success of government policy, then all concepts of justice can go out of the window. Happiness economics has an egotistic, hedonistic, individualistic bias, argues Vos, which also has nothing to do with morality.

Boettke and Coyne have several objections to the interventionist conclusions of many happiness proponents. Any one of these objections would be problematic for the interventionists but, together, they are surely fatal. The idea that the happiness of individuals can be measured and aggregated so that public policy can maximise happiness is surely impractical. Furthermore, happiness measures across time must be of doubtful value. Back in the early nineteenth century, people would not have had cures for infectious diseases or anaesthetics for operations. They would also not have known that they could exist. As such, people might well have had measured happiness just as great as we have 150 years later. Are we seriously claiming that our wellbeing was just as great without these innovations – and would have remained just as great without them?

This takes us to the important topic of the different forms of wellbeing, something that is also discussed by other authors. Innovation and economic growth, for example, may not improve emotional wellbeing but they will improve life satisfaction. Unfortunately, these are two distinct concepts and policies will have different effects on the two measures. How do we trade off an improvement in emotional wellbeing with a fall in life satisfaction? Surely, this is not something that the government can do for a single individual, let alone aggregate across the whole of society.

Boettke and Coyne also observe that the happiness proponents completely overlook the subject of public choice economics when making policy proposals. Self-interested officials who are not omniscient will ensure that we do not get anything close to optimal public policy. Indeed, there is a great irony. Those happiness economists who propose public policy interventions make great play of the fact that people seek status as a positional good. It is the cause of many of the problems they seek to fix with their policies. Those who implement interventionist policies to promote happiness, however, will have high status. Furthermore, the more interventions they successfully recommend the higher their status will be. Incentives will not be very well aligned in such circumstances! So what should the approach to policy be in this area? The government should focus on creating the meta-framework of institutions that *give us the freedom to flourish and improve our wellbeing.* In other words the government should not be trying to 'maximise happiness' but facilitating *the pursuit of happiness.* This is especially important given that there is no general agreement about the meaning of happiness and because wellbeing takes different forms which people will want to trade off in different ways.

Pedro Schwartz, in the final chapter, also takes a philosophical view. He correctly defines the agenda of the happiness policy activists as a utilitarian agenda – indeed, this is the self-declared position of economists such as Richard Layard. Schwartz starts by suggesting that a complex society cannot be organised according to one overriding ethical principle – the maximisation of happiness. The values that we pursue in small groups are also not appropriate for organising a large society. During wartime, there may be a single agreed goal and society is organised – with a certain loss of liberty – towards meeting that goal. During normal times, this approach is not appropriate. Indeed, if it is agreed that society has only one goal – that of maximising wellbeing – then the process of government becomes an operational research problem: how to best govern society to maximise measured wellbeing.

The reader may consider that this is knocking down a straw man and that nobody seriously believes that societies should be centrally planned to maximise happiness, just as nobody really believes these days in centrally planning an economy to maximise wealth. Many of the utilitarians in the happiness debate, however, do believe in strong government intervention to achieve their goals. Furthermore, if the complete planning of society is not possible because planners cannot have all the information that would be necessary to achieve their objective, then partial planning is surely impossible too. Even the most benign wellbeing advocates desire policy interventions because they believe that those interventions will increase the happiness of some members of society more than they will decrease the happiness of others. Indeed, if the wellbeing advocates in central government do not believe that central government policy decisions can lead to greater aggregate happiness, then why are they even collecting the relevant data?

Schwartz's attack on other aspects of Layard's agenda is also important. Layard regards leisure as a form of public good – or, at least, as having positive externalities. He therefore wants work to be heavily taxed. Furthermore, when we earn more money we not only make ourselves happier but make our neighbours less happy as they fall behind in relative terms. Schwartz responds: 'My conclusion is that the happiness economics that Lord Layard has built on utilitarian foundations elevates envy to the category of a public virtue, endangers political liberty and shackles social progress.' Schwartz further argues that, even if leisure does carry positive externalities, the rationale for government intervention, given what Coase and also public choice economics have taught us, is very limited.

Schwartz's final criticism invokes Hayek; it is subtle but important. In the small group, as part of the process of evolution, we have learned to respond to pleasure and pain. The Great Society (to use Hayek's term) has evolved in that context. This does not create, however, in any way, a case for the Great Society adopting the maximisation of pleasure (net of pain) as its governing principle. What sort of actions might maximise the pleasure of people within a given country? Possibly they would be cruel punishments for criminals, strict immigration controls, the protection of local businesses ... and so on. In the small group, we might be suspicious of outsiders at first – that is how networks of trusting people often develop – but, if that translates into a 'wellbeing' policy to keep outsiders out of the country because the Office for National Statistics finds that this increases measured happiness, then the Great Society will be jeopardised. Indeed, Schwartz concludes largely as Boettke and Coyne conclude – the policy approach must be one of creating the overarching framework of personal freedom so that we can – as individuals and groups – freely pursue our wellbeing.

In conclusion, it is to be hoped that, when the Office for National Statistics concludes its studies, it will set great store by Bjørnskov's empirical conclusions – backed up in less direct ways by the authors of other chapters in this monograph. Countries that inhibit the freedom of their citizens to a lesser degree have happier citizens. Paradoxically, therefore, wellbeing may be maximised if the government does not consciously try to pursue that objective specifically. This should not be surprising. The wellbeing policy activists accuse economists of focusing too much on the maximisation of national income as a government policy objective. This is a false accusation, but a lesson can be drawn from attempts by government to increase national income. It also happens to be the case that economic growth is higher when governments do not specifically plan for that end. In other words, the central planning of a society to achieve a particular desired end is likely to fail to meet that end, as well as changing completely the nature of the society.

This is not to say that some useful policy advice cannot be found from the empirical work on happiness economics. It can tell us, for example – though we probably knew already – that policies that impede employment seriously affect wellbeing. Those authors whose chapters deal with the normative issues, however, make a very strong case in this monograph that government policy should not promote wellbeing explicitly.

PART ONE: GDP OR GWB?

2 THE FOLLY OF WELLBEING IN PUBLIC POLICY

Paul Ormerod

Introduction

The idea that government policy should be focused more explicitly on promoting happiness – or wellbeing; the two terms are used interchangeably – has been gaining support. For example, in the UK in April 2011 the Office for National Statistics began to include subjective wellbeing monitoring questions in their regular Integrated Household Survey to capture what people think and feel about their own wellbeing. This was in response to a public consultation on the issue of measuring wellbeing launched by Prime Minister David Cameron in November 2010.

Proponents of this view argue that happiness indicators, based on surveys which purport to measure how happy people feel, have stagnated over decades. And the key reason, they argue, is because governments have paid far too much attention to maximising a narrowly defined, materially based measure of economic welfare, gross domestic product (GDP),[1] rather than a more holistic indicator of welfare. This premise is clearly false.

One of the most disturbing tendencies in the happiness

---

1 Gross national product (GNP) is sometimes used instead, particularly in the USA. There are some marginal differences between the two concepts which are not in practice important; the two measures are very similar, especially in terms of growth rates over time.

literature is the belief that experts know better what is good for people. Better not just than elected politicians, but better than the voters themselves. So, for example, Derek Bok, a former president of Harvard, states in his book *The Politics of Happiness* that 'people are surprisingly bad judges of what makes them happy'. The implication is that decisions on policy can safely be left, indeed they *ought* to be left, to the so-called expert, armed with a clipboard and some multiple regression analysis.

The main purpose of this chapter is to illustrate important points which we can learn from the experience over more than half a century of trying to measure and control GDP. The scholars who first measured GDP realised from the outset that it had serious limitations. Indeed, that there is no unique, scientifically correct way of measuring it. The same point applies to the happiness data, yet it is scarcely recognised by the proponents of happiness-based policies. Despite the serious limitations of the GDP data, little time was lost by governments in trying to predict and control the future path of GDP. Gordon Brown's notorious statement, when he was British Chancellor of the Exchequer, that he would 'abolish boom and bust', was merely one example of a whole litany of attempts since World War II to engineer misguided policies based on this belief. The same holds true of the happiness data, where identical arguments on both the ability and desirability of predicting and controlling it are being made.

The GDP 'straw man'

Economics has undoubtedly been important in post-war political life, not just in Britain, but across the Western world as a whole. But Bill Clinton's famous aphorism, 'It's the economy, stupid!', has not always been a decisive factor in determining the outcome of elections. Indeed, despite the benign world economic environment which coincided with the Clinton presidency – reasonable growth of GDP, rising employment, low inflation – his own Democratic Party lost the election in 2000. In Britain, the Conservatives under Margaret Thatcher were re-elected in 1983 with an increased majority, despite the 1980–82 recession being the deepest since World War II, in which unemployment rose from around one million to over three million. With John Major in charge, the Conservatives won the 1992 general election following the recession of 1990/91, but were overwhelmingly defeated by Tony Blair in 1997 after several years of very strong economic growth from 1993 onwards, accompanied by sharp falls in unemployment, inflation and interest rates.

Despite the straw man erected by wellbeing advocates, politicians *do* exhibit concerns over a wide range of issues where GDP is not the immediate focus. For example, in many European countries at the moment, both the level of future immigration and the degree to which existing immigrants ought to integrate with their host cultures are very live issues which no serious politician can afford to ignore. Business leaders may attempt to turn the matter into a purely economic one, arguing that immigration helps them, but this is certainly not how it is seen by large sections of the European electorates. Crime is another topic of perennial interest to voters. Its relative importance fluctuates over time, but again politicians respond by trying to either shape or appease the prevailing public mood. It is always an issue which they must address.

Yes, economics and economic policy matter to voters, but so do other issues, and it is wholly misleading to suggest that policy is focused solely on the maximisation of GDP, or indeed that it is given far too much weight compared to other policy objectives.

Even under the control of Gordon Brown, a politician who would have been perfectly at home as commissar of the Five Year Plan in the old Soviet Union, grinding out endless and meaningless statistics on tractor production, the British Treasury placed great emphasis on this point. The official British government guidelines on policy appraisal, the Treasury's *Green Book*,[2] clearly states: 'wider social and environmental costs and benefits for which there is no market price also need to be brought into any [policy] assessment' and that the inclusion of 'non-market impacts is a challenging but important element of appraisal, and should be attempted wherever feasible'.

GDP as a concept does not capture these wider costs and benefits. But this is not because economists are so stupid or narrow-minded as to ignore them. The simple fact is that GDP was never intended to include them in the first place. The purpose of inventing and constructing the so-called national accounts, in which GDP is a key feature, was precisely to measure the value of the output of an economy, as far as possible using market-based prices to do so.

Simon Kuznets was a highly original economist who undertook distinguished work in a number of areas and received the Nobel Prize in 1971. He was the seminal figure in working out how to measure output – GDP – in a systematic way some three decades previously. He and his colleagues knew at the time that there was more to life than the workings of a market-oriented economy. In his Nobel lecture,[3] for example, Kuznets specifi-

---

2   Her Majesty's Treasury, *Green Book: Appraisal and Valuation in Central Government*, 2003, available on the Treasury website.

3   S. Kuznets, 'Modern economic growth: findings and reflections', Nobel Prize

cally discussed the social implications of growth and argued that: 'Many of these are of particular interest, because they are not reflected in the current measures of economic growth; and the increasing realization of this shortcoming of the measures has stimulated lively discussion of the limits and limitations of economic measurement of economic growth.'

GDP was measured in the first place because, at the time, output was by far the most serious concern of policymakers. Specifically, they were focused on the massive collapses in economic activity which took place in the Great Depression in the early 1930s. In the financial crisis of 2008/09, output fell by some 3 per cent in America and 5 per cent in Germany. There is a widespread perception that things were pretty bad. But in the 1930s, GDP collapsed by nearly 30 per cent in both, and nearly one in every four men was unemployed.

There was a pressing need to provide policymakers with information on what was happening to output. So the specific focus was on measuring output in economies in which activity mainly took place in markets. Even then, many sectors were not part of an explicit market, including most of the public sector, with defence being a prime example. How do we measure the output of our defence forces, when we simply cannot trade them in a market and see what they are worth? Gradually over time, international conventions have emerged on how to deal with these problems. They do not avoid the problem that there is a certain degree of arbitrary judgement involved, but there is now a broad consensus on how to deal with such issues.

The question of measuring non-market output is conceptually

Lecture, 1971, available at: www.nobelprize.org/nobel_prizes/economics/laureates/1971/kuznets-lecture.html.

different from that of happiness and wellbeing, but it is often confused with them in practice. Namely: should we, and if so how, extend the concept of GDP to include more 'non-market' factors? Here again, economists have not been the laggards, but have been at the very forefront of the debate. As long ago as 1971, for example, the distinguished American economists Bill Nordhaus and James Tobin constructed estimates of GDP which took into account environmental factors. Intriguingly, their title was 'Is growth obsolete?' (Nordhaus and Tobin, 1971). So perhaps there is nothing new under the sun after all!

A wide range of further adjustments to the basic measure of GDP have been suggested, such as weighting income by the degree of inequality, deducting the value of 'bads' such as time spent commuting, valuing work in the house, and so on. While the possibility of obtaining a consensus on whether and how to value such things is somewhat higher than it was 40 years ago when Nordhaus and Tobin first wrote, any such adjustments inevitably involve a fairly high degree of arbitrary judgement. GDP, for all its faults, has a clear theoretical basis and, for the most part, an unequivocal meaning.

Wellbeing and measures of economic and social progress

The wellbeing movement goes far beyond tinkering with what is and what is not included in GDP, even when the adjustments might be substantial. It suggests replacing it altogether with a measure which purports to describe not the material prosperity of a population, but its happiness.

Surveys on the levels of happiness reported by individuals

have been carried out over a few decades in most Western countries. The recorded levels of happiness fluctuate from year to year, but in general there is no apparent trend, either up or down. Over the same period, average material standards of living, measured by real GDP per head, have shown a very clear upward trend.

This finding is repeated endlessly and appears to have made an impression on many people. We see the level of happiness over time rumbling along showing no obvious trend. By contrast, there is GDP per head bounding ahead, soaring into the stratosphere. As a result, many people believe that 'money does not buy you happiness'.

Time series data do indeed appear to show that nations do not get happier over time as they get richer. In contrast, happiness is positively correlated with individual income within a given country at any point in time: the rich generally report greater happiness than the poor. This, the so-called Easterlin paradox, named after the doyen of happiness studies, Richard Easterlin, is also discussed at length in the happiness literature. An implication which is widely drawn is that if we do not get happier as we get richer, this effect must be due to the pernicious psychological effects of inequality.

These findings are used to recommend 'progressive' policies in the name of equality, such as progressive tax rates and wealth redistribution. Griffith (2004), for example, in the *Boston College Law Review*, stated that 'happiness research is consistent with the strongest justification for adopting a progressive tax structure'. This may be thought an obscure journal, but a Google search of the phrase 'Griffiths progressive taxation' yields 91,900 sites and the article has generated a large literature. In the UK, the New Economics Foundation is one of many bodies which base their calls for higher, more progressive taxes on the 'science' of happiness. Richard Layard, one of the leading academic proponents of happiness, argues that progressive taxation will make society unequivocally better off from the perspective of happiness.

The fact that measured happiness has not increased over decades is viewed by some commentators as indicating a flaw in our society which must be corrected through government intervention. Happiness supporters believe that they occupy the perceived moral high ground as a result of such findings. As a result, it appears to them that increasing happiness is a self-evident good, to which only the most irredeemable misanthrope could object.

But we can also compare trends in measured happiness over time with factors other than income. Figure 1, for example, shows happiness and real public expenditure in the UK from 1979 to 2010. These factors are measured on quite different scales, so to make the comparison of their progress over time easier to see, the values of each of them in 1979 have been set equal to 100. This does not mean that they were in any sense the same in that year; it is just a useful and standard way of comparing over time two series which are naturally measured in different units.

And in Figure 2 we can see happiness and the degree of inequality (using the standard concept of the Gini coefficient to measure the latter), again with both set equal to 100 in 1979.

If rising GDP has no effect on happiness, as is alleged, what do we conclude from these two charts?[4] Increasing public spending in real terms (i.e. after allowing for inflation) by some 60 per cent has made no difference to the wellbeing of the nation. So

4   Invoking multiple regression rather than simple correlation does not affect the message here.

Figure 1 **Happiness and public expenditure in the UK, 1979–2010**

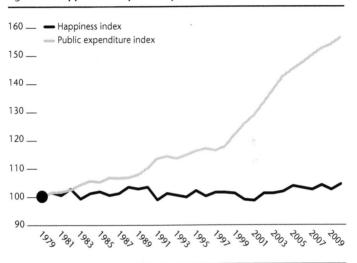

Figure 2 **Happiness and inequality in the UK, 1979–2010**

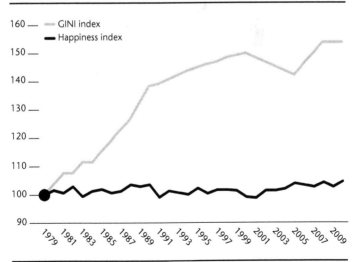

presumably we should not be interested in increasing public expenditure, using exactly the same argument which is used in the context of GDP and happiness. Further, we should be indifferent to rising income inequality, because this appears to have no effect on happiness.

The basic message of the two charts, it should be said, is not confined to the UK but is qualitatively similar across many Western countries. And this lack of correlation extends to a wide range of variables. For example, using UK data from 1973 onwards, there is no correlation between self-reported life satisfaction and either real current public expenditure or lower hours of work. In the USA, life expectancy for whites rose from 71.7 years in 1970 to 78.4 in 2007 (the latest year for which estimates are available). For blacks, the increase was even higher, from 64.1 to 73.6, representing not merely an absolute rise, but a narrowing of the gap with whites. Gender inequality as measured by the median earnings of women compared with men has fallen sharply. In 1970, women earned 59.4 per cent of men's earnings, rising to 77.0 per cent in 2009. Yet there was no correlation between happiness and any of these improvements.

We could indeed conclude from this flat trend that attempting to improve the human lot through *any* policy – not just through pursuing economic growth – is entirely futile. Alternatively, we could conclude that happiness data over time show little movement because they do not have much meaning. The evidence points to the latter.

Inherent weaknesses in happiness measures

There are very good reasons why happiness measured in this way is flat. When happiness is measured, people are asked to register their level of happiness on a scale of n categories (e.g. 1 = 'not happy', 2 = 'fairly happy' or 3 = 'very happy'). These numbers are then averaged over the population to gain an overall happiness score. Discrete categories mean that people have to undergo large discrete change in their happiness in order for this to be registered by the indicator: and once they have reached the top category they officially cannot experience any further increase in their happiness. As a consequence, noticeable changes in average happiness can come about only through substantial numbers of people moving category.

As a general rule, if the happiness of 1 per cent of the population (net) increases enough for them to place themselves in the next category, the average happiness score increases by 0.01. For example, happiness surveys on a three-category scale in the USA typically yield an average happiness of about 2.2. In order for the happiness measure to undergo a 10 per cent increase, 22 per cent of the population would have to undergo a substantial enough increase in their happiness for them to be shunted up to the next category. Any happiness-inducing event would have to be of long duration, not be offset by countervailing trends in society, and the individual could not have adapted to it if the change is to be perceptible in the data over time.[5]

It is very difficult to think of a set of circumstances in which 22 per cent of the population would find themselves moving from, say, 'fairly' to 'very' happy over the space of a few years. It is

---

5 These points were made by Helen Johns in a mathematical supplement to Johns and Ormerod (2008). Johns also makes the point that, for the US data, the sampling error of the data is comparable to or larger than any movement in the indicator caused by real changes in average happiness.

therefore not surprising that we observe average happiness to be sluggish compared with other social or economic indicators such as GNP.

Furthermore, *by construction*, the happiness data can exhibit no indefinite trend. As individuals answer a survey in which they are asked to state their own level of happiness on an n-point scale, the data is bounded between one and n. Over any particular short period of time, an apparent trend either up or down might exist, but by definition it cannot persist. In contrast, at least as it is presently defined, real GNP can exhibit no upper bound. Indeed, for the past 200 years it has shown a persistent trend increase.

This difference in the trends, or the lack of them, in different data series does, incidentally, raise very serious theoretical problems about interpreting any sort of correlation, simple or multiple, between variables such as happiness which have no trend by construction and others which do such as GDP. The technical mathematical level of these concepts is high, with Clive Granger and Robert Engle winning the Nobel Prize in economics for their contribution. Interested readers are referred in the first place to the Wikipedia entry on 'cointegration'.[6]

The relationship between happiness and income revisited

More subtle recent work is in fact suggesting that there is a clear and positive connection between life satisfaction and income, and that there appears to be no cut-off point to this. Satisfaction continues to grow with higher income even at very high levels.

---

6   http://en.wikipedia.org/wiki/Cointegration.

Even though the extra satisfaction gained per unit of additional income becomes smaller as income rises, it is nevertheless an increase.

Daniel Kahneman is a psychologist who was awarded the Nobel Prize in economics in 2002 for his work on how people actually behave rather than how they are assumed to behave in economic theory. His colleague at Princeton, Angus Deaton, is a former president of the American Economic Association. In 2010, they published a paper in the *Proceedings of the National Academy of Sciences*[7] which distinguishes two aspects of wellbeing. First, life satisfaction, defined as the thoughts which people have about their life when they think about it. Secondly, emotional wellbeing, which refers to the emotional quality of an individual's everyday experience, the frequency and intensity of emotions such as joy, anger and sadness. They analysed a database containing 450,000 responses by Americans to a range of questions.

The results of Kahneman and Deaton are striking. Life satisfaction is unequivocally related in a positive way to income, but emotional wellbeing is not. Deaton had previously challenged the 'happiness' consensus of a lack of connection between wellbeing and GDP in a paper published in the *Journal of Economic Perspectives* (Deaton, 2008). He showed, using data from countries around the world, that life satisfaction continued to rise with income, in a similar way to the relationship found in the subsequent study with Kahneman.

The widespread view, based upon looking at charts of data over time and backed up by fairly simple statistical analysis, that there is no connection between GDP and happiness over

---

7   See Kahneman and Deaton (2010): www.pnas.org/cgi/doi/10.1073/pnas.1011492107.

time appears to be challenged by these recent studies, which take a more sophisticated analytical approach. GDP does appear to continue to have wider value as an indicator of a successful society, over and above its direct purpose of measuring material prosperity. As an aside there has long been a view that it is only *above* a certain level of income that individuals and societies can really begin to flourish, to enjoy the full fruits of civilisation. For example, Aneurin Bevan, the left-wing Labour politician who founded the National Health Service in 1948, was fond of stating 'Freedom is the by-product of economic surplus'.

Controlling economic and social life to 'promote happiness'

Neither the recent empirical evidence nor the more general philo-sophical considerations have prevented happiness advocates from continuing to insist that a single measure of happiness should be the only way of evaluating policy and progress. This is despite the fact, as already noted, that the way in which the aggregate happi-ness indices are constructed means that there is not only, by defi-nition, an absolute upper limit to the value they can take, but that it requires major shifts of attitude by large numbers of people to make any appreciable difference to the index.

The problem is not merely that this lobby wants to replace GDP with a happiness index. It is the belief that, by measuring happiness, it then becomes subject to prediction and control by policymakers. Claims are made that the drivers of aggregate happiness, the factors that cause the index to move, are well understood and therefore should become the levers of policy.

The happiness literature contains very little firm evidence on the factors which seemingly cause happiness. The ones which are best established in the literature are those that have a more traditional orientation in policy terms, such as being married or having a religious faith. But curiously, we rarely see happiness experts vigorously promoting these as aims of policy.

We can't predict GDP either ...

Of course, it is always possible that further research will provide stronger and more settled evidence on the factors that generate movements in the overall measures of happiness. We might usefully reflect, however, on the experience of GDP in this respect.

The immediate motive for constructing estimates of GDP was, quite simply, to provide more information on what was happening to output, by far the most important aspect of domestic policy at the time. Once armed with this data, however, it was quite natural for researchers to begin to investigate whether relationships could be discovered which enable us to understand why GDP moved as it did over time. And these relationships could then be used for prediction (for example, would there be another recession next year?) and policy control (if a recession is predicted, by changing policy now can we can prevent it from happening?).

Indeed, very quickly, models of the economy appeared, based on relationships estimated by techniques drawn from the new science of econometrics, the application of statistical theory to the particular technical issues raised by economic data. Lawrence Klein was an American economist and econometrician who was awarded the Nobel Prize in 1980 for his pioneering work in this field. As early as 1947, he published an econometric model of the

US economy with the title 'The use of econometric models as a guide to economic policy' (see Klein, 1947).

So the process of measuring the economy metamorphosed almost overnight into the desire to use these measurements to predict and control it, exactly as is the case with happiness today.

Enormous optimism was expressed about these possibilities, despite the salutary experience of the spectacular failures of forecasts carried out in the summer of 1945 for the rest of that year and for 1946. Klein himself documented the errors in an article (see Klein, 1946). Unemployment, for example, had been forecast to be 8 million but was only 3 million. But he argued that output could be predicted much more accurately, and that the correct application of econometrics to this data meant that 'we can look forward to much better results in the post-transition period'.

Over 60 years on, we have a massive literature on all the nuances of economic forecasting, spanning a wide range of statistical techniques and economic theories, far more sophisticated than the highly innovative but rather crude methods of Klein in the 1940s. But it is no exaggeration to say that no progress has been made in the accuracy of forecasts. At key times, the onsets of booms or recessions, forecasts prove just as inaccurate as they were in 1945. The *Bank of England Quarterly Bulletin* in October 2008, for example, shows that the consensus forecast for UK and US GDP growth in 2009 in January 2008 was for positive growth of 2.0 and 2.7 per cent respectively. As late as August, the forecasts were still for positive growth, despite the fact that by then both economies were in recession and output was already falling! The actual out-turn for 2009 was negative growth of 3 per cent in America and 5 per cent in Britain. There are many such examples.

It is not just that we cannot predict the economy with

any reasonable level of systematic accuracy. We still have no consensus as to what the drivers of GDP are, and therefore what the effects of any particular policy might be, even in a qualitative sense. At the time of writing, for example, one school of thought, of which Joe Stiglitz is a prominent member, believes that more fiscal expansion is required to revive growth in the US and European economies. Another school, in which Robert Barro is prominent, maintains that fiscal expansion will actually lead to lower economic activity.

Of course, the fact that economics has made little or no progress in its ability to predict and control the macroeconomy does not necessarily mean that the same fate awaits the happiness index and its devotees. Changes in both real GDP and happiness over time share a deep common feature, however. Namely, that they are, across the Western world as a whole, scarcely indistinguishable from purely random series. There is a small amount of pattern, of potential information, in the US GDP data, but it is small. And, more generally, these data series are dominated by random noise rather than by any consistent 'signal'.[8]

Conclusion

This experience with GDP has a critical implication. It is simply not possible to obtain systematically reliable predictions of aggregate happiness indices, any more than it is for GDP. We cannot predict with accuracy the next shake of a true die, and neither can we do so for happiness. Further, any statistical relationship which purports to identify the drivers of happiness (or GDP) over time

---

8   Interested readers are referred to Ormerod and Mounfield (2000).

will be essentially illusory, whatever statistical validation tests are applied to the sample data, and will break down and cease to be valid. This is not merely a theoretical point. It is the entire experience of the history of macroeconomic modelling.

Indeed, government attempts to increase measured happiness, rather than making life better for us, may well actually do the opposite. They will create arbitrary objectives which divert civil service energies from core responsibilities; give many people the message that happiness emanates from national policy rather than from our own efforts; and they will create pressure for government to appear to increase an indicator which has never before shifted systematically in response to any policy or socio-economic change.

These are exactly the mistakes of the target-driven mentality which has come to pervade the British public sector more generally. We should learn from these mistakes rather than replicate them.

More sinisterly, the happiness view of the world has tendencies which are inherently anti-democratic. The expert with his or her clipboard and regressions *knows* better than ordinary people themselves what makes them happy. By this presumption of knowledge, local democratic or individual decisions can be overridden with a clean conscience. Not all decisions are made at the Department for Motherhood and Apple Pie, so a happiness objective glosses over the very real 'tough choices' which policymaking entails.

GDP is not an all-encompassing measure of welfare; it simply measures the size of the economy. There are many things important to our wellbeing which are not captured by it. Those things need to be sustained by a strong civil society and a democratically accountable, well-run government. If we cannot make convincing cases for them without 'scientific proof' that they make people happy, we are totally morally adrift. Government does not fail because it does not measure happiness; it fails when its energies are misdirected on the basis either of poor-quality information or of the false presumption of knowledge by would-be central planners.

References

Deaton, A. (2008), 'Income, health and wellbeing around the world: evidence from the Gallup world poll', *Journal of Economic Perspectives*, 22(2): 53–72.

Griffith, T. D. (2004), 'Progressive taxation and happiness', *Boston College Law Review*, 45(5): 1363–1398.

Johns, H. and P. Ormerod (2008), 'The unhappy thing about happiness economics', *Real-World Economics Review*, 46: 139–46.

Kahneman, D. and A. Deaton (2010), 'High income improves evaluation of life but not emotional well-being', *PNAS*, 107(38): 16489–16493

Klein, L. R. (1946), 'A post-mortem on transition predictions of national product', *Journal of Political Economy*, LIV: 289–307.

Klein, L. R. (1947), 'The use of econometric models as a guide to economic policy', *Econometrica*, 15: 111–151.

Layard, R. (2005), *Happiness: Lessons from a new science*, Harmondsworth: Penguin.

Nordhaus, W. D. and J. Tobin (1971), 'Is growth obsolete?', Cowles Foundation Discussion Papers 319, Cowles Foundation for Research in Economics, Yale University.

Ormerod, P. and C. Mounfield (2000), 'Random matrix theory and the failure of macroeconomic forecasting', *Physica A*, 280: 497–504.

3 SUBJECTIVE WELLBEING, INCOME, ECONOMIC DEVELOPMENT AND GROWTH

Daniel W. Sacks, Betsey Stevenson and Justin Wolfers

Introduction

Does economic growth improve the human lot?[1] Using several data sets which collectively cover 140 countries and represent nearly all of the world's population, we study the relationship between subjective wellbeing and income, identifying three stylised facts. Firstly, we show that, within a given country, richer individuals report higher levels of life satisfaction. Secondly, we show that richer countries on average have higher levels of life satisfaction. Thirdly, analysing the time series of countries that we observe repeatedly, we show that, as countries grow, their citizens report higher levels of satisfaction. Importantly, we show that the magnitude of the relationship between satisfaction and income is roughly the same across all three comparisons, which suggests that absolute income plays a large role in determining subjective wellbeing.

These results overturn the conventional wisdom that there is no relationship between growth and subjective wellbeing. In a series of influential papers, Easterlin (1973, 1995, 2005a, 2005b) has argued that economists' emphasis on growth is misguided, because he finds no statistically significant evidence

---

1   This chapter is adapted from Sacks et al. (2010). In turn, that paper clarified and simplified many of the findings originally described in Stevenson and Wolfers (2008).

of a link between a country's GDP and the subjective wellbeing of its citizens. This is despite the fact that Easterlin and others (e.g. Layard, 1980) have found that richer individuals in a given country report higher levels of wellbeing. Researchers have reconciled these discordant findings, together called the Easterlin paradox, by positing that wellbeing is determined by relative, rather than absolute, income. By this view, individuals want only to keep up with the Joneses. If true, the Easterlin paradox suggests that focusing on economic growth is futile: when everyone grows richer, no one becomes happier. A related concern, voiced for example by Di Tella and MacCulloch (2010), is that subjective wellbeing adapts to circumstance. If correct, this argument implies that long-run growth makes people no better off because their aspirations and expectations grow with their income. A third concern is that, even if wellbeing rises with income for the very poor, individuals eventually reach a satiation point, above which further income has no effect on wellbeing (Layard, 2005). Yet in this paper, we present evidence that wellbeing rises with absolute income: full stop. This evidence suggests that relative income, adaptation and satiation are of only secondary importance.

Subjective wellbeing is multifaceted: it includes both how happy individuals are at a point in time and how satisfied they are with their lives as a whole (Diener, 2006). Throughout this chapter, we focus on life satisfaction, which is the variable that is both most often measured and has been the focus of much of the existing literature (even as economists have often referred to these satisfaction questions as measuring 'happiness'). Although life satisfaction is the focus of this paper, we consider a variety of alternative measures of subjective wellbeing and show that they also rise with income.

Main findings

Our first finding is that richer individuals are more satisfied with their lives, and that this finding holds across 140 countries, and several data sets. Across each of these countries, the relationship between income and satisfaction is remarkably similar. Our graphical analysis suggests that subjective wellbeing rises with the log of income. This functional form implies that a 20 per cent rise in income has the same impact on wellbeing regardless of the initial level of income: going from $500 to $600 of income per year yields the same impact on wellbeing as going from $50,000 to $60,000. This specification is appealing on theoretical grounds because a standard assumption in economics is that the marginal impact of a dollar of income diminishes as income increases.

We then look at cross-country evidence. Using larger data sets than previous authors have examined, we find an economically and statistically significant relationship between average levels of satisfaction in a country and the log of GDP per capita. The data also show no evidence of a satiation point. Whereas Easterlin (1974) had argued that the relationship between wellbeing and income seen within countries was stronger than the relationship seen between countries, and that this provided evidence for the importance of relative income, our evidence undermines the empirical foundation for this claim.

Time-series evidence is then examined. While the within-country and between-country comparisons cast doubt on the Easterlin paradox, they do not by themselves tell us whether economic growth in fact translates into gains in subjective wellbeing. This question has challenged researchers for some time because of a lack of consistent time-series data on subjective wellbeing. We analyse the time-series movements in subjective wellbeing using two sources of comparable repeated cross-national cross-sections. Each data set spans over two decades and covers dozens of countries. In analysing the time-series data we can subject the hypothesis that wellbeing depends on relative income to a test: if notions of a good life change as the income of one's fellow citizens grows, then we should see only a modest relationship between growth in satisfaction and growth in average income, relative to our point-in-time estimates. This is because the general growth in income does not make people feel better. However, we present economically and statistically significant evidence of a positive relationship between economic growth and rising satisfaction over time, although limited data mean that these estimates are less precise than our other findings.

Finally, we turn to alternative measures of subjective wellbeing, showing that they too rise with a country's income. We find that happiness is positively related to per capita GDP across a sample of 69 countries. We then show that additional, effect-specific measures of subjective wellbeing, such as whether an individual felt enjoyment or love, or did not feel pain, are all higher in countries with higher per capita GDP. Our finding that subjective wellbeing rises with income is therefore not confined to an unusual data set or a particular indicator of subjective wellbeing.

Background on subjective wellbeing

Subjective wellbeing has many facets. Some surveys, such as the World Values Survey, ask respondents about their life satisfaction, asking, 'All things considered, how satisfied are you with your life these days?' The Gallup World Poll includes a variant of this question in which respondents were shown a picture and told

'Here is a ladder representing the "ladder of life." Let's suppose the top of the ladder represents the best possible life for you; and the bottom, the worst possible life for you. On which step [between 0 and 10] of the ladder do you feel you personally stand at the present time?' This question, which we refer to as the satisfaction ladder, is a form of Cantril's 'Self-Anchoring Striving Scale' (Cantril, 1965). Other surveys ask about happiness directly. Gallup also asks a battery of more specific questions, ranging from 'Were you proud of something you did yesterday?' to 'Did you experience a lot of pain yesterday?' Whereas the satisfaction question invites subjects to assess the entirety of their wellbeing, the more specific questions measure feelings rather than assessments (Diener, 2006). In this chapter, we largely focus on life satisfaction.

We do this for two reasons. First, we would like to use as many data sets as possible to assess the relationship between subjective wellbeing and income. It is the case that income and life satisfaction and the satisfaction ladder are more commonly measured than any other measure. Secondly, the previous literature documenting the Easterlin paradox (including Easterlin 1974, 1995, 2005a, 2005b, 2009) has largely focused on life-satisfaction questions (even though researchers have tended to label these analyses of 'happiness'). As noted above, we do then look at other measures of wellbeing and find the results are similar to the income–satisfaction link.

Subjective wellbeing data are useful only if the questions succeed in measuring what they intend to measure. Economists have traditionally been sceptical of subjective data because they lack any objective anchor and because some types of subjective data suffer from severe biases (e.g. Diamond and Hausman, 1994). These objections apply to subjective wellbeing data, but a variety of evidence points to a robust correlation between answers to subjective wellbeing questions and alternative measures of personal wellbeing. For example, self-reported wellbeing is correlated with physical measures such as heart rate and electrical activity in the brain as well as sociability and a propensity to laugh and smile (Diener, 1984). Self-reported wellbeing is also correlated with independently ascertained friends' reports and with health and sleep quality (Diener et al., 2006; Kahneman and Krueger, 2006). Measures of subjective wellbeing also tend to be relatively stable over time and they have a high test–retest correlation (Diener and Tov, 2007).

Subjective wellbeing data lack a natural scale and are reported differently across data sets. For example, happiness questions often ask respondents to choose a level of happiness from 'very happy' to 'very unhappy', with one or two nominal values in between. Life satisfaction can be measured on a similar scale, or on a ladder of life with ten or eleven rungs. In order to compare answers across surveys, we convert all subjective wellbeing data into normalised variables, subtracting the sample mean and dividing by the sample standard deviation. Whenever we report the subjective wellbeing–income gradient, therefore, we are effectively reporting the average number of standard deviation changes in subjective wellbeing associated with a one-unit change in income (or log income). This rescaling has the disadvantage of assuming that the difference between any two levels of life satisfaction is equal, although in fact the difference between the fifth and sixth rung on the ladder of life may be very different from the difference between the ninth and the tenth. Stevenson and Wolfers (2008) show, however, that the results discussed here are robust to alternative approaches.

Within-country estimates of the satisfaction–income gradient

We begin our study of life satisfaction and income by comparing the reported satisfaction of relatively rich and less rich individuals in a given country at a point in time. Many authors have found a positive and strong within-country relationship between subjective wellbeing and income. For example, Robert Frank argues as follows: 'When we plot average happiness versus average income for clusters of people in a given country at a given time ... rich people are in fact a lot happier than poor people. It's actually an astonishingly large difference. There's no one single change you can imagine that would make your life improve on the happiness scale as much as to move from the bottom 5 percent on the income scale to the top 5 percent' (Frank, 2005: 67). We confirm this relationship and, taking advantage of the enormous size of many of our data sets, estimate precisely the magnitude of the within-country satisfaction–income gradient.

We assess the relationship between satisfaction and income by estimating 'lowess regressions' of satisfaction against the log of household income. Lowess regression effectively estimates a separate bivariate regression around each point in the data set, but weights nearby points most heavily (Dinardo and Tobias, 2001). Traditional regression analysis imposes a linear relationship, while the lowess procedure allows researchers to study the functional form of the relationship between two variables – in this case, for example, between life satisfaction and the log of income.

In Figure 3, we plot the lowess estimate of the relationship between the satisfaction ladder score and the log of household income for each of the largest 25 countries in the world, using data

Figure 3   **Relationship between wellbeing and income, within individual countries: Gallup World Poll**

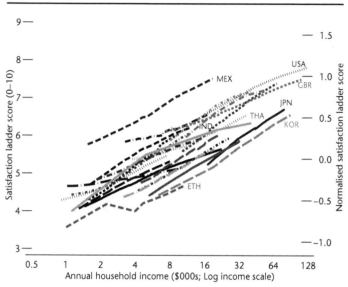

Note: The satisfaction data are shown both on their raw (0–10) scale on the left axis, and as standardised variables on the right axis. We plot the lowess fit between the 10th and 90th percentiles of each country's income distribution. Selected countries only have been marked – see Annexe on p. 94 for country code key, which applies for all figures.

from the Gallup World Poll.[2] Satisfaction scores are shown both as their raw (0–10) scores on the left axis, and in their standardised form (obtained by subtracting the whole sample mean and dividing by the standard deviation) on the right axis.

Figure 3 reveals the well-known finding that richer citizens of a given country are more satisfied with their life. For most countries, this plot reveals that satisfaction rises linearly with the log

2   We are using a more recent vintage of the Gallup World Poll than Stevenson and Wolfers (2008), incorporating data made available through 13 October 2008.

of income (as the horizontal axis is on a log scale). Moreover, the gradient is similar across countries, with the estimated lines for each country looking like parallel shifts of each other. In spite of the enormous differences between these countries the relationship between income and life satisfaction is remarkably similar. Finally, we note that this figure provides no evidence of satiation. While some have argued that, above a certain point, income has no impact on wellbeing, in these countries we see that the curve is just as steep at high levels of income as at low levels. While these 25 countries account for the majority of the world's population, Gallup polled individuals in 132 countries, making their poll the widest survey of subjective wellbeing ever undertaken. We can therefore take our analysis further.

More comprehensive wellbeing surveys

Of these 132 countries, 126 had income data that could be used in our analysis. We therefore examined the relationship between wellbeing and income by pooling data from all the countries in our data sets, and we estimated regressions from them. These results are presented in column 1 of Table 1,[3] and described in detail in Sacks et al. (2010). Here we describe the results briefly together with related results using the first four waves of the World Values Survey which spans 1980–2004 and asks respondents to assess their life satisfaction on a 1–10 scale. We also consider the relationship between wellbeing and income using the 2002 Pew Global Attitudes Survey, which covers 44 countries at all levels of development and uses the same ladder of life question as Gallup.

---

3   Table 1 is in the Annexe to this chapter, on page 94.

From these different data sets, the estimated satisfaction–income gradient ranges from 0.216 in the World Values Survey to 0.281 in the Pew Global Attitudes Survey. Within a given country, at a point in time, people with higher income tend to report greater life satisfaction. One problem with these results, however, is that differences in income between individuals within a country reflect both transitory and permanent differences (and each has different implications for subjective wellbeing). For example, somebody on a low income might be a senior executive between jobs. On the other hand, income differences between countries, which will be discussed below, are likely to be much more persistent, and indeed close to entirely permanent.

We need to begin by considering how much of the cross-sectional variation in income within a country represents variation in permanent income. Standard estimates for the USA suggest that around two-fifths to a half of the cross-sectional variation in *annual* income comes from variations in permanent income and the rest amounts to transitory differences (Haider, 2001; Gottschalk and Moffit, 1994).[4] Our survey asks about *monthly* income and the transitory share will be larger. To be conservative, we simply choose the upper end of the estimates of the transitory share of income. We also need to convert the variation in transitory income into its permanent income equivalent. If each extra dollar of transitory income persists for only one year, then people would be indifferent between one extra dollar of transitory income and a rise in permanent income of about five cents (assuming a 5 per cent discount rate). Estimates of the transitory

---

4   Our calculations will use these US estimates as if they are representative of the entire world, though what is really needed is similar studies for countries at different levels of development.

component of annual income suggest that it does not all dissipate in one year; indeed, the auto-regressive process estimated by Haider (2001) suggests that the permanent income equivalent of a $1 rise in transitory income would be about twice the one-year value, or ten cents. Consequently a $1 increase in income in the cross-section represents, on average, a 50 cent rise in permanent income, plus a 50 cent rise in transitory income, and this transitory income is valued as equivalent to a rise in permanent income of about five cents.

This means that the rise in permanent income from a given change in recorded income is less than the change in recorded income. As such, the underlying relationship between wellbeing and permanent income is going to be even stronger than the relationship between wellbeing and recorded income. To interpret our estimated wellbeing–income gradient in terms of a $1 rise in permanent income, our cross-sectional estimates should be scaled up by about 80 per cent (1/0.55). We do this adjustment and report the new coefficients in column 2. We find a higher gradient for the relationship between wellbeing and our estimates of the log of permanent income of a little over 0.4. Overall, our reading of the within-country evidence is that the life satisfaction-log to permanent income gradient falls between 0.3 and 0.5.

We should not push these adjustments too hard, however. While it seems straightforward to think that permanent rather than transitory income determines subjective wellbeing, in fact direct evidence on this point suggests the opposite: subjective wellbeing and the business cycle move quite closely together. Stevenson and Wolfers (2008) report that the output gap strongly predicts subjective wellbeing, at least in the USA. Wolfers (2003) shows this also holds in Europe and across states in the USA.

International comparisons of satisfaction and income

The within-country relationship between income and life satisfaction is well known and can lead to at least two interpretations. The first interpretation is that greater earning capacity makes people more satisfied with their lives. Higher income allows people to purchase more healthcare, enjoy more leisure time, eat fancier food and so on; people may also be freed from financial stress. A second interpretation, however, is that people care less about money than about having money relative to some reference point (Easterlin, 1973). One reference point is their neighbour's income, but other reference points include a country (or the world's) average income. Or perhaps people use their own previous income as a reference point. Under this view, people are stuck on a 'hedonic treadmill': as they grow richer, their expectations adapt to their circumstances, and they end up no more satisfied than they were before (Brickman and Campbell, 1990). An alternative is that an 'aspiration treadmill' means that even as higher income yields greater wellbeing, people may eventually report no higher wellbeing than they previously reported because their expectations grow with their income and wellbeing.

To sort out these interpretations, we turn to national data. If all that matters for satisfaction is one's own income relative to one's neighbour's income, or relative to mean national income, then people in countries with high average income should be no more satisfied than people in poorer countries. Alternatively, to the extent that national differences in income reflect long-lasting differences, individuals should adapt to them (if adaptation is important), so adaptation predicts that the cross-country satisfaction–income gradient should be small. On the other hand, if absolute income matters (or if the relevant reference point is mean global income), we would expect richer countries indeed to be more satisfied. Thus we now assess the satisfaction–income gradient across countries.

Our measure of average income in a country is GDP per capita, measured at purchasing power parity, to adjust for international differences in price levels. These data come from the World Bank's World Development indicators database. Where we are missing data, we turn to the Penn World Tables (version 6.2), and, failing that, the CIA Factbook. For earlier years for which data are unavailable, we use Maddison (2007).

The World Values Survey contains within it some data problems, such as the wellbeing survey not being representative in some countries. Typically, they tend to miss out groups that might be expected to have low satisfaction. This survey shows a general pattern of wellbeing increasing with income: the countries with the unrepresentative wellbeing data, however, do not tend to follow the general pattern. It is also true that the early waves of the survey, which contain mostly wealthy nations, provide only suggestive, but not overwhelming, evidence for a positive link between the log of GDP per capita and subjective wellbeing. A researcher who mistakenly included the non-representative countries and who plotted satisfaction against the level rather than the log of income could well (erroneously) fail to find a statistically significant relationship between GDP per capita and subjective wellbeing. Successive waves of the survey included more middle- and low-income countries, and the relationship between income and wellbeing is clearer in those later waves. The four waves span 25 years and 79 distinct countries, with income ranging from less than $1,000 to over $32,000 (in 2000 international US dollars).

There is a clear and approximately linear-log relationship

Figure 4   Life satisfaction and real GDP per capita: Gallup World Poll

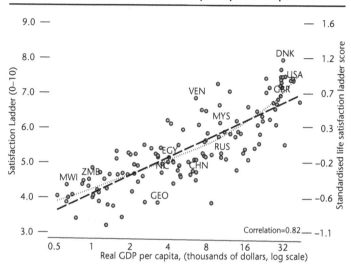

Note: Selected countries only have been marked.

between life satisfaction and GDP using this World Values Survey. Other data sets employing alternative measures of satisfaction show a similar positive relationship. Data from the Pew Global Attitudes Survey show the same pattern as data from the World Values Survey with richer countries exhibiting higher levels of satisfaction.

Satisfaction seems to grow with log income at about the same rate, whether we focus on rich countries or poor countries. There is no evidence that the satisfaction-log–income gradient diminishes as income grows, suggesting that no country is rich enough to have hit a satiation point, if such a point exists.

The Gallup World Poll has the greatest coverage. In Figure

4, we plot the satisfaction ladder scores against per capita GDP for 131 countries included in the Gallup World Poll (we exclude Palestine, because we were unable to find reliable GDP data). Every part of the GDP distribution is well represented. This figure confirms the by-now strong impression that richer countries have higher levels of life satisfaction than poorer countries and that this relationship is approximately log-linear. Indeed, the correlation between average satisfaction scores in a country and its log of GDP per capita is above 0.8.

Because average wellbeing is rising as a function of the *log* of average income, our results suggest that transferring a given amount of money from rich to poor countries could raise life satisfaction, because $100 is a larger percentage of income in poor countries than rich countries. The linear-log relationship revealed by the non-parametric fits also provides evidence against satiation: the relationship between wellbeing and income does not diminish at high levels of income, except to the extent implied by the log functional form. If anything, the lowess curve appears to tick upwards even more sharply at high levels of GDP.

More detailed analysis

We quantify the magnitude of the satisfaction–income link by running regressions that analyse the satisfaction of individuals in a given country as a function of the log of average per capita income in their own country. We then aggregate our satisfaction data up into national averages and run regressions that show by how much average satisfaction in a country increases (in terms of number of standard deviations) when the log of average per capita income in a country is higher.

These results, in column 2 of Table 1, confirm the graphical analysis: all three of our data sets show a statistically significant and positive relationship between satisfaction and the log of GDP. These results suggest that absolute income plays an important role in explaining the relationship between satisfaction and income. The magnitude of the relationship is similar whether we estimate it using individual-level data or are looking at the relationship between national average wellbeing and income levels. It is also similar whether or not we adjust for the differential age and sex composition of respondents. The coefficients on the log of average income vary somewhat but are centred on the range 0.3 to 0.4.

This range is striking for its resemblance to the within-country satisfaction–income gradient. The relationship between wellbeing and income across countries is very similar to the relationship between wellbeing and income within given countries. Across the 126 countries with valid income data, we find that there is no country with a statistically significant negative relationship between satisfaction and income, and the relationship between satisfaction and income for each country is of the same direction and has a similar slope to the relationship between satisfaction and income across countries. In other words, our estimates of the satisfaction–income gradient are similar whether estimated within or between countries.

Recall that the Easterlin paradox rested on the belief that the relationship between wellbeing and income was stronger within countries than between countries. Earlier estimates of statistically insignificant cross-country relationships between average satisfaction and average income reflected the fact that previous researchers were looking at small samples of fairly homogeneous countries. It was the juxtaposition of this statistically insignificant finding with evidence of a statistically significant wellbeing–income relationship within countries which led Easterlin to declare that the paradox existed. *But the historical absence of evidence for a proposition – that richer countries are happier – should not have been confused as being evidence of its absence.* Indeed, with our larger data sets, we find statistically significant evidence that high-income countries are happier than their low-income counterparts. In fact, a claim about the importance of relative income comparisons should rest upon the quantitative magnitudes of the estimated relationships between wellbeing and income. Indeed, further work by Stevenson and Wolfers (2010) concludes that relative income plays at best a minor role in determining life satisfaction.

An alternative story is based on the idea that people adapt to their income level. By this view, what matters for satisfaction is income relative to expectations. Higher income does not make us happier because we adapt. Furthermore, variations in income that have persisted for sufficiently long for expectations to adapt should therefore be unrelated to satisfaction. The differences in income between countries are lasting. Indeed, across the 131 countries in the Gallup World Poll, the correlation between the log GDP per capita in 2006 and its value in 1980 is 0.93. If people adapt to changes in income so that long-lasting changes in income do not make them happier, persistent cross-country differences in GDP per capita should have little explanatory power for satisfaction. The data clearly falsify this hypothesis.

Satisfaction and economic growth

So far we have shown that richer individuals report higher life satisfaction than poorer individuals in a given country, and that, on average, citizens of rich countries are more satisfied with their lives than are citizens of poor countries. These comparisons suggest that absolute income plays an important role in determining wellbeing, but they do not directly address our central question: does economic growth improve subjective wellbeing?

We answer this question by turning to the time-series evidence on life satisfaction and GDP, which allows us to assess whether countries that experience economic growth also experience growth in subjective wellbeing. Estimating the time-series relationship between GDP and subjective wellbeing is difficult because sufficiently comparable data are rarely available. For example, the General Social Survey in the USA and the Life in Nation surveys in Japan both surveyed subjective wellbeing over a long horizon, but both are afflicted by important changes in the wording and ordering of questions that, if not recognised, can lead to serious interpretation errors.

Nevertheless, many scholars have found that the USA has not got any happier over the past 35 years despite becoming wealthier. As Stevenson and Wolfers (2009) note, there is also a somewhat puzzling decline in female happiness. In contrast, Japan, which was once thought to have experienced little increase in happiness over the post-war period, has, in fact, experienced significant happiness gains that are similar in magnitude to those one would expect given the cross-sectional and cross-country relationships between subjective wellbeing and income. These happiness gains become apparent, however, only once changes in the survey over time are taken into account (Stevenson and Wolfers, 2008); the failure to take account of these changes had led many previous scholars astray (including Easterlin, 1995, 2005a).

We draw on two long-running data sets to examine the relationship between subjective wellbeing and economic growth: the World Values Survey and the Eurobarometer. We analyse the first four waves of the World Values Survey, which span 1980 to 2004 and cover 79 distinct countries. Because the World Values Survey added many countries in later waves, however, it is not possible to make many comparisons of a given country.[5] The Eurobarometer survey has the advantage that it has been surveying people in member nations of the European Union continually since 1973; it has the disadvantage, however, of covering only relatively homogeneous countries. Unlike the other surveys, Eurobarometer ascertains life satisfaction on a four-point scale.[6]

Nine countries were included in the original Eurobarometer sample. Analysing data to 1989, Easterlin (1995) concluded that the data failed to show any relationship between life satisfaction and economic growth. In Figure 5, we present scatter plots of life satisfaction and the log of GDP per capita for the nine countries Easterlin analysed. In the figure we include as dark circles the original data he analysed; hollow circles denote data that have subsequently become available through to 2007. The dark circles by themselves do not always show a strong relationship; over the full sample, however, eight of the nine countries show a positive

5   As noted earlier, some of the country samples in earlier waves of the World Values Survey are not directly comparable with later waves since their survey frames were (intentionally) not nationally representative. Our analysis focuses only on nationally representative samples.

6   For the analysis, we keep West Germany and East Germany as separate countries. For further details on the Eurobarometer and our data procedures, see Stevenson and Wolfers (2008).

Figure 5   Changes in life satisfaction and economic growth in Europe: Eurobarometer Survey

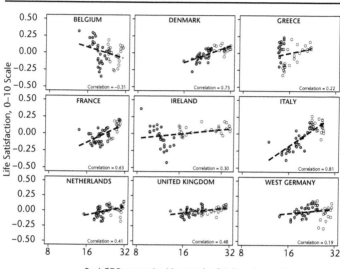

Real GDP per capita (thousands of dollars, log scale)

Notes: Data are aggregated by first standardising individual-level data to have mean zero and unit standard deviation, and then taking country-year averages of the standardised values. The life satisfaction question asks, 'On the whole, are you very satisfied, fairly satisfied, not very satisfied, or not at all satisfied with the life you lead?'

relationship between life satisfaction and growth, and six of the nine slopes are statistically significantly positive. The slopes range from −0.25 in Belgium to 0.68 in Italy. This reanalysis not only suggests a positive relationship between income and growth, but also hints at the difficulty of isolating this relationship when data are scarce.

The positive relationship between life satisfaction and economic growth is not a feature of Europe alone. The World Values Survey covers more countries, and at very different levels of development. This allows us to see whether populations become more satisfied as their countries transition from low to moderate income as well as from moderate to high income. The evidence from this data suggests that there is a positive association between changes in subjective wellbeing and changes in income. It also seems clear, however, that life satisfaction is more sensitive to short-run changes in income than to long-run changes, suggesting that business-cycle variation may be driving some of the association. An alternative interpretation is that, over time, individuals adapt to their new circumstances or their aspirations change, so that, even though their material welfare is increasing their subjective wellbeing, gains from these increases recede over time.

There are also some interesting outliers from an examination of the broader data. Korea, for example, had only a modest change in subjective wellbeing and a very large increase in GDP; Hungary experienced very little growth, but had a serious decline in life satisfaction. In the regression results reported below, we include these outliers, but it is clear that excluding them could change our estimates. Overall, our work provides strong evidence of a relationship between economic growth and growth in wellbeing. The satisfaction–income gradient is 0.51 in the World Values Survey and 0.17 in the Eurobarometer, as we report in column 3 of Table 1. Our data reject the hypothesis that it is relative rather than absolute income which determines wellbeing. The results are not substantially affected by outliers.

In obtaining these estimates, however, we have drawn on all the variation in GDP in our sample, including possibly high-frequency changes to which individuals do not have a chance to adapt. If adaptation occurs slowly, it would be better to focus on long-run changes in GDP. Indeed, Easterlin and Angelescu (2009) argue that only long-run economic growth can be used to assess the relationship between growth and wellbeing.

We can assess long-run differences for all countries by comparing changes in satisfaction and national income between the first and the last time we observe a country in the World Values Survey. For the countries in the World Values Survey that we observe multiple times, the average difference in time between first and last observations is about eleven years. This is comparable with Easterlin and Sawangfa's notion of the 'long run' – they require data spanning at least ten years – but a little lower than Easterlin and Angelescu's twelve-year requirement. It appears from this analysis that, for most countries, GDP and satisfaction move together. There is, nevertheless, a notable number of countries for which life satisfaction and GDP move in opposite directions. Even so, the correlation between life satisfaction and GDP is positive and remarkably strong. Looking at the long-run data overall, once again we cannot reject the hypothesis that the true coefficient explaining the relationship between satisfaction and national income is between 0.3 and 0.4.

The influence of the transition economies

Using these same data (although including the observations from the unrepresentative national samples and not adjusting for wave fixed effects), Easterlin and Sawangfa (2008: 13) argue that 'the positive association between the change in life satisfaction and that in GDP per capita reported by Stevenson and Wolfers rests almost entirely on the positively correlated V-shaped movement of the two variables during the post-1990 collapse and recovery

Figure 6   Long differences in life satisfaction and log GDP,
World Values Survey

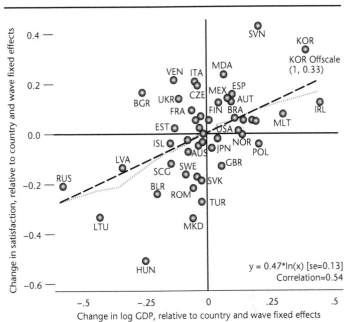

Note: Data are aggregated by first standardising individual-level data to have mean zero and unit standard deviation, and then taking country-year averages of the standardised values. Selected countries only have been marked.

in the transition countries'. In order to investigate this claim, we separately estimated our panel regressions and long differences for the sample of transition countries only and then for all other World Values Survey nations. While breaking the sample apart like this reduces our statistical precision, the key inferences remain the same in both samples: the influence of GDP growth on satisfaction is positive, statistically significantly different from zero, and we cannot reject our conclusion that these coefficients lie between 0.3 and 0.4. Indeed, if anything, the World Values Survey yields estimates of the satisfaction–income gradient that are somewhat larger. The critique levelled by Easterlin and Sawangfa seems, quite simply, wrong.

Figure 6 provides further evidence of why estimating the relationship between subjective wellbeing and long-run growth has challenged researchers. There are many countries which do not fit the general trend that growth in satisfaction is correlated with GDP growth. Bulgaria, Ukraine, Venezuela and Estonia all experienced considerable declines in income, with no accompanying decline in wellbeing. Furthermore, a researcher, worried about outliers, could easily drop a handful of influential countries from the sample – such as Russia, Hungary, Slovenia and Korea. Doing so clearly does not eliminate the positive correlation, but it does substantially reduce the statistical power of the regression, because these extreme cases involve so much of the variation in GDP. When we exclude these countries from our regression of long-run differences, our estimate of the relationship between satisfaction and GDP growth remains positive and comparable with other estimates at 0.26, but the standard error grows to 0.15.

Results using the Eurobarometer data

This exercise was also repeated using the Eurobarometer data. The advantage of these data is that we have many observations for each country which we can combine to reduce the influence of measurement error. Thus we construct long-run differences in the Eurobarometer by taking averages of satisfaction and log GDP for each country in each of the decades 1973–82, 1983–92, 1993–2002

Figure 7   Decadal differences in life satisfaction and log GDP: Eurobarometer

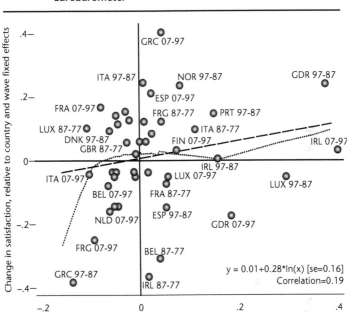

Note 1: The dashed line gives the ordinary least squares (OLS) fit and the dotted line is fitted from lowess regression. Selected countries only have been marked.
Note 2: The figures '87', '97' etc. denote the mid points of the two decades for which differences are taken.

and 2003–07. We then construct decadal differences in satisfaction and GDP by comparing adjacent decades and plot these decadal differences in Figure 7; we report the regression estimates in Table 1, column 4. Each point represents a single decadal difference in satisfaction and GDP for a given country. Many countries experienced sluggish income growth but no relative slowdown in subjective wellbeing: most of these countries are in western

Europe. For a majority of countries, however, GDP and satisfaction do move in the same direction, although the correlation is much weaker than in our previous estimates. The estimated satisfaction–income gradient resulting from these long-run differences is marginally statistically significant at 0.28.

Conclusion on wellbeing and economic growth

Overall we find a positive but somewhat less precise relationship between growth in subjective wellbeing and growth in GDP. When we use all of the time-series variation in GDP, we find a relationship between wellbeing and income that is similar to the within-country and cross-sectional gradients. When we estimate longer-run differences, the precision of the relationship falls but the point estimate is similar in magnitude. This remains true whether we exclude potentially problematic 'transition' economies from the sample or not, or whether we limit our attention to long-run changes in income or not, or whether we analyse data from the World Values Survey or the Eurobarometer. None of our estimates using the full variation in GDP allows us to reject the hypothesis that the gradient lies between 0.3 and 0.4, the range of our estimates of the static relationship between wellbeing and income.

Alternative measures of subjective wellbeing

Thus far, we have shown that there is a positive, statistically significant and quantitatively important relationship between life satisfaction and income. This satisfaction–income gradient is similar in magnitude whether one analyses individuals in a given country,

Figure 8   Happiness and GDP: World Values Survey, 1999–2004

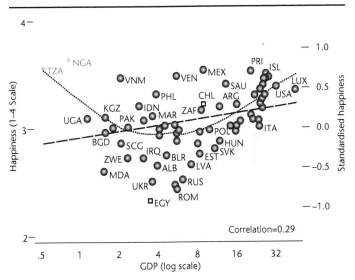

Notes: The happiness question asks: 'Taking all things together, would you say you are: "very happy," "quite happy," "not very happy," [or] "not at all happy"?' The dashed line plots fitted values from the reported OLS regression (including TZA and NGA); the dotted line gives fitted values from lowess regressions. Observations represented by hollow squares are drawn from countries in which the World Values Survey sample is not nationally representative. Selected countries only have been marked.

in countries at a point in time or in a given country over time. But life satisfaction is not the only measure of subjective wellbeing, and so we now turn to considering the relationship between various other measures of subjective wellbeing and income. For brevity (and also owing to data availability), we will focus on cross-country comparisons of these alternative indicators.

In Figure 8 we begin by showing the cross-sectional relationship between happiness and the log of GDP per capita, using data from the fourth wave of the World Values Survey. We follow the same conventions as in previous charts, showing the national averages both as their average on their original four-point scale, and as standardised values (on the right-hand-side axis). We also show both the regression line (where the dependent variable is the standardised measure of happiness) and the non-parametric fit; this regression line shows a positive and statistically significant relationship between happiness and per capita GDP, although the estimated happiness–income gradient is not as large as the satis-faction–income gradient we estimated above. The presence of two extreme outliers, Tanzania and Nigeria, skews the regression estimates considerably. These countries are particularly puzzling because they are the poorest in the sample, but they report among the highest levels of happiness. They also have much lower average life satisfaction – indeed, Tanzania is the least satisfied of any country in our sample. Perhaps there is a banal explanation for this puzzle: survey documentation suggests that there are difficul-ties translating the happiness question in Tanzania. Stevenson and Wolfers (2008) discuss the happiness–income link more fully and find very similar results to the satisfaction–income link: happiness increases at any aggregation of the data, and the magnitude of the link is not affected to any great extent by the degree of aggregation.

We turn now to alternative and more specific measures of subjective wellbeing. The Gallup World Poll asks respondents about many facets of their emotional health and daily expe-rience. For several experiences, such as enjoyment, physical pain, worry, sadness, boredom, depression, anger or love, the Gallup poll asks: 'Did you experience [feeling] during a lot of the day yesterday?' These questions sketch a psychological profile of hundreds of thousands of people spanning the world's income distribution. In Figure 9, we present scatter plots of the

Figure 9   **Cross-country measures of recalled feelings and GDP: Gallup World Poll**

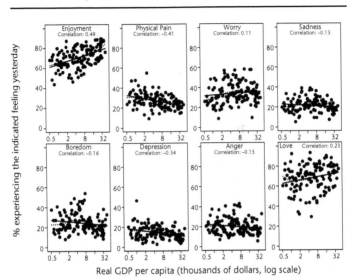

Notes: Each observation represents one of up to 130 developed and developing countries in the sample (questions were not asked in Iraq). Dashed lines are fitted from ordinary least squares regressions of the percentage agreeing with the statement on log real GDP per capita; dotted lines are fitted from lowess estimations.

probability that an individual in a given country experienced various emotions yesterday, against GDP per capita. The figure suggests that citizens of richer countries are more likely to experience positive emotions and less likely to experience negative emotions. Enjoyment is very highly correlated with GDP, while love is moderately correlated. Physical pain, depression, sadness and anger all decline moderately with GDP.[7] Worry increases

---

7   See Krueger et al. (2010) for a more thorough exploration of the relationship between experiencing pain and income.

slightly with GDP, although there is not a strong pattern.

The Gallup poll also probes respondents for an array of sentiments about their day yesterday, asking whether they: felt well rested; were treated with respect; chose how to spend their time; if they smiled or laughed a lot; were proud of something they did; or ate good-tasting food. The daily experience questions, which uniformly measure positive experiences, paint a picture that is consistent with our analysis thus far. People in richer countries are more likely to report feeling better rested and respected, smiling more and eating good-tasting foods than people in poorer countries, although they are no more likely to take pride in what they did or to have learned something interesting.

These data point to a more nuanced relationship between wellbeing and income. While they give no reason to doubt that wellbeing rises with income, they also suggest that certain facets of wellbeing respond less to income than others. These data hint at the possibility of understanding which emotions and experiences translate into that part of life satisfaction which is sensitive to changes in income.

Conclusions

This paper revisits the stylised facts on the relationship between subjective wellbeing and income. We find that, within a given country, rich individuals are more satisfied with their lives than poorer individuals and we find that richer countries have significantly higher levels of average life satisfaction. Studying the time series relationship between satisfaction and income, we find that economic growth is associated with increases in life satisfaction.

The key innovation in this chapter is to focus explicitly on the magnitude of the subjective wellbeing–income gradient (rather than its statistical significance), while also bringing the greatest quantity of data to bear on these questions. We show that the within-country, between-country and over-time estimates all point to a quantitatively similar relationship between subjective wellbeing and income. This relationship is robust: we find it not only at different levels of aggregation but using different data sets. We also find that income is positively associated with other measures of subjective wellbeing, including happiness as well as other upbeat emotions.

The fact that life satisfaction and other measures of subjective wellbeing rise with income has significant implications for development economists. First, and most importantly, these findings cast doubt on the Easterlin paradox and various theories suggesting that there is no long-term relationship between well-being and income growth. Absolute income appears to play a central role in determining subjective wellbeing. This conclusion suggests that economists' traditional interest in economic growth has not been misplaced. Secondly, our results suggest that differences in subjective wellbeing over time or across places are likely to reflect meaningful differences in actual wellbeing.

Subjective wellbeing data therefore permit cross-country wellbeing comparisons without reliance on price indices. As Deaton (2010) notes, if we wish to use some kind of dollar-a-day threshold to count poverty, then we need price indices that account for differences in quality and in quantity of consumption in different countries. In practice, these are difficult to construct. Instead we can use wellbeing data. Deaton notes that these comparisons using wellbeing data are valid only if life satisfaction responds to absolute rather than relative wellbeing. If individuals assess their life relative to contemporary standards, then as countries and the world grow richer, reported satisfaction may not change. Our analysis suggests, however, an important role for absolute income in determining life satisfaction; therefore we conclude that subjective wellbeing data is indeed likely to be useful in assessing trends in global wellbeing.

Finally, we should note that we have focused on establishing the magnitude of the relationship between subjective wellbeing and income, rather than on disentangling causality from correlation. The causal impact of income on individual or national subjective wellbeing, and the mechanisms by which income raises subjective wellbeing, remain open and important questions.

References

Brickman, P. and D. T. Campbell (1990), 'Hedonic relativism and planning the good society', in M. H. Appley (ed.), *Adaptation Level Theory: A Symposium*, New York: Academic Press.

Cantril, H. (1965), *The Pattern of Human Concerns*, New Brunswick, NJ: Rutgers University Press.

Deaton, A. (2010), 'Price indexes, inequality, and the measurement of world poverty', *American Economic Review*, 100(1): 5–34.

Di Tella, R. and R. MacCulloch (2010), 'Happiness adaption to income beyond "basic needs"', in E. Diener, J. Helliwell and D. Kahneman (eds), *International Differences in Well-being*, New York: Oxford University Press.

Diamond, P. A. and J. A. Hausman (1994), 'Contingent valuation: is some number better than no number?', *Journal of Economic Perspectives*, 8(4): 45–64.

Diener, E. (1984), 'Subjective well-being', *Psychological Bulletin*, 95(3): 542–75.

Diener, E. (2006), 'Guidelines for national indicators of subjective well-being and ill-being', *Journal of Happiness Studies*, 7(4): 397–404.

Diener, E. and W. Tov (2007), 'Culture and subjective well-being', in S. Kitayama and D. Cohen (eds), *Handbook of Cultural Psychology*, New York: Guilford.

Diener, E., R. E. Lucas and C. N. Scollon (2006), 'Beyond the hedonic treadmill: revising the adaptation theory of well-being', *American Psychologist*, 61(4): 305–14.

Dinardo, J. and J. L. Tobias (2001), 'Nonparametric density and regression estimation', *Journal of Economic Perspectives*, 15(4): 11–28.

Easterlin, R. A. (1973), 'Does money buy happiness?', *The Public Interest*, 30: 3–10.

Easterlin, R. A. (1974), 'Does economic growth improve the human lot? Some empirical evidence', in P. A. David and M. W. Reder (eds), *Nations and Households in Economic Growth: Essays in Honor of Moses Abramowitz*, New York: Academic Press.

Easterlin, R. A. (1995), 'Will raising the incomes of all increase the happiness of all?', *Journal of Economic Behavior and Organization*, 27(1): 35–48.

Easterlin, R. A. (2005a), 'Feeding the illusion of growth and happiness: a reply to Hagerty and Veenhoven', *Social Indicators Research*, 74(3): 429–33.

Easterlin, R. A. (2005b), 'Diminishing marginal utility of income? Caveat emptor', *Social Indicators Research*, 70(3): 243–55.

Easterlin, R. A. (2009), 'Lost in transition: life satisfaction on the road to capitalism', *Journal of Economic Behavior and Organization*, 71(1): 130–45.

Easterlin, R. A. and L. Angelescu (2009), 'Happiness and growth the world over: time series evidence on the happiness–income paradox', IZA Discussion Paper no. 4060.

Easterlin, R. A. and O. Sawangfa (2008), 'Happiness and economic growth: does the cross section predict time trends? Evidence from developing countries', IZA Discussion Paper no. 4000.

Frank, R. H. (2005), 'Does absolute income matter?', in P. L. Port and L. Bruni (eds), *Economics and Happiness: Framing the Analysis*, Oxford: Oxford University Press.

Gottschalk, P. and R. Moffit (1994), 'The growth of earnings instability in the U.S. labor market', *Brookings Papers on Economic Activity*, 1994(2): 217–54.

Haider, S. J. (2001), 'Earnings instability and earnings inequality of males in the United States: 1967–1991', *Journal of Labor Economics*, 19(4): 799–836.

Kahneman, D. and A. B. Krueger (2006), 'Developments in the measurement of subjective well-being', *Journal of Economic Perspectives*, 20(1): 3–24.

Kahneman, D., A. B. Krueger, D. Schkade, N. Schwarz and A. A. Stone (2006), 'Would you be happier if you were richer? A focusing illusion', *Science*, 312(5782): 1908–10.

Krueger, A., B. Stevenson and J. Wolfers (2010), 'A world of pain', Mimeo, University of Pennsylvania.

Layard, R. (1980), 'Human satisfaction and public policy', *Economic Journal*, 90(363): 737–50.

Layard, R. (2005), *Happiness: Lessons from a new science*, London: Penguin.

Luttmer, E. F. P. (2005), 'Neighbors as negatives: relative earnings and well-being', *Quarterly Journal of Economics*, 120(3): 963–1002.

Maddison, A. (2007), 'Historical statistics for the world economy: 1–2003 AD', www.ggdc.net/maddison/Historical_Statistics/horizontal-file_03–2007.xls.

Sacks, D. W., B. Stevenson and W. Wolfers (2010), 'Subjective well-being, income, economic development and growth', National Bureau of Economic Research Working Paper 16441.

Stevenson, B. and J. Wolfers (2008), 'Economic growth and subjective well-being: reassessing the Easterlin Paradox', *Brookings Papers on Economic Activity*, 2008(1): 1–87.

Stevenson, B. and J. Wolfers (2009), 'The paradox of declining female happiness', *American Economic Journal: Economic Policy*, 1(2): 190–225.

Stevenson, B. and J. Wolfers (2010), *Inequality and Subjective Well-being*, Working paper.

Wolfers, J. (2003), 'Is business cycle volatility costly? Evidence from surveys of subjective well-being', *International Finance*, 6(1): 1–26.

Annexe

Table 1 **Regression results from several data sets**

Dependent variable: standardised life satisfaction	Within-country, cross-person regression	Cross-person, income adjusted	Cross-country regression	Long-difference time series regressions
Gallup World Poll: ladder question	0.232*** (0.014)	0.422	0.342*** (0.019)	–
World Values Survey: life satisfaction	0.227*** (0.037)	0.413	0.370*** (0.036)	0.505*** (0.109)
Pew Global Attitudes Survey: ladder question	0.283*** (0.027)	0.515	0.204*** (0.037)	–
Eurobarometer: life satisfaction	–	–	–	0.278* (0.164)

Note: The table reports the coefficient on the log of household income (in column 1) or GDP (otherwise), obtained from regressing standardised life satisfaction on the indicated measure of income using the indicated dataset. ***, ** and * denote statistically significant at 1 per cent, 5 per cent and 10 per cent, respectively. For more details, see Sacks et al. (2010), especially Tables 1–3.

Listing of country names and abbreviations

Afghanistan	AFG	Argentina	ARG
Angola	AGO	Armenia	ARM
Albania	ALB	Australia	AUS
United Arab Emirates	ARE	Austria	AUT
		Azerbaijan	AZE

Burundi	BDI	Spain	ESP
Belgium	BEL	Estonia	EST
Benin	BEN	Ethiopia	ETH
Burkina Faso	BFA	Finland	FIN
Bangladesh	BGD	France	FRA
Bulgaria	BGR	West Germany	FRG
Bosnia and Herzegovina	BIH	Great Britain	GBR
		East Germany	GDR
Belarus	BLR	Georgia	GEO
Bolivia	BOL	Ghana	GHA
Brazil	BRA	Greece	GRC
Botswana	BWA	Guatemala	GTM
Canada	CAN	Hong Kong	HKG
Switzerland	CHE	Honduras	HND
Chile	CHL	Croatia	HRV
China	CHN	Haiti	HTI
Cameroon	CMR	Hungary	HUN
Colombia	COL	Indonesia	IDN
Costa Rica	CRI	India	IND
Cuba	CUB	Ireland	IRL
Cyprus	CYP	Iran	IRN
Czech Republic	CZE	Iraq	IRQ
Germany	DEU	Iceland	ISL
Denmark	DNK	Israel	ISR
Dominican Republic	DOM	Italy	ITA
Algeria	DZA	Jamaica	JAM
Ecuador	ECU	Jordan	JOR
Egypt	EGY	Japan	JPN

Kazakhstan	KAZ	Nicaragua	NIC
Kenya	KEN	Northern Ireland	NIR
Kyrgyzstan	KGZ	Netherlands	NLD
Cambodia	KHM	Norway	NOR
South Korea	KOR	Nepal	NPL
Kuwait	KWT	New Zealand	NZL
Laos	LAO	Pakistan	PAK
Lebanon	LBN	Panama	PAN
Sri Lanka	LKA	Peru	PER
Lithuania	LTU	Philippines	PHL
Luxembourg	LUX	Poland	POL
Latvia	LVA	Puerto Rico	PRI
Morocco	MAR	Portugal	PRT
Moldova, Republic of	MDA	Paraguay	PRY
Madagascar	MDG	West Bank and Gaza Strip	PSE
Mexico	MEX		
Macedonia	MKD	Romania	ROM
Mali	MLI	Russian Federation	RUS
Malta	MLT	Rwanda	RWA
Myanmar	MMR	Saudi Arabia	SAU
Montenegro	MNE	Serbia and Montenegro	SCG
Mozambique	MOZ		
Mauritania	MRT	Senegal	SEN
Malawi	MWI	Singapore	SGP
Malaysia	MYS	Sierra Leone	SLE
Niger	NER	El Salvador	SLV
Nigeria	NGA	Serbia	SRB
		Slovakia	SVK

Slovenia	SVN	Ukraine	UKR
Sweden	SWE	Kosovo	UNK
Chad	TCD	Uruguay	URY
Tonga	TGO	United States	USA
Thailand	THA	Uzbekistan	UZB
Tajikistan	TJK	Venezuela, Bolivarian Rep. of	VEN
Trinidad and Tobago	TTO		
Turkey	TUR	Vietnam	VNM
Taiwan, China	TWN	Yemen, Republic of	YEM
Tanzania, United Republic of	TZA	South Africa	ZAF
		Zambia	ZMB
Uganda	UGA	Zimbabwe	ZWE

4 ARE MORE EQUAL COUNTRIES HAPPIER?
Christopher Snowdon

Happiness is flatlining

A graph which shows nothing happening for fifty years is not the most auspicious starting point for a radical theory. In spite of wars, recessions, oil crises, inflation and the fluctuating fortunes of the nation's football teams, self-reported happiness in Britain has resolutely refused to budge. When the crime rate rocketed, it remained as flat as a bowling green; when the crime rate fell, it displayed not a flicker of satisfaction. Religions withered, diseases were cured, politicians came and went, interest rates rose and fell, but nothing would sway the population's happiness from its horizontal march. Whether people are questioned about happiness, life satisfaction or social wellbeing,[1] there has been very little change in the nation's mood since the 1960s – which is to say, since the questionnaires were first drawn up on a regular basis.

National happiness surveys offer little hope to anyone wishing to demonstrate that anything has made people more cheerful in the last half-century. For those wishing to prove that something has *not* made us happier, on the other hand, the relentless straight line can embellish almost any narrative. It could, for example, be used to demonstrate the futility of pursuing health as

---

1   Although there are some differences between these three measures, the results remain much the same and I will use the terms interchangeably.

a political objective given that the ten-year increase in life expectancy enjoyed by the average Briton since 1965 has apparently not led to greater happiness. Equally, it could be argued that neither women's liberation nor the expansion of the welfare state has improved the human lot.

Such arguments are almost never put forward. Instead, it is always the assertion that economic growth has failed to boost wellbeing which has dominated debate. This debate began when Richard Easterlin first noticed the paradox of rising GDP and flatlining happiness in the USA in 1974. The Easterlin paradox has since been challenged by researchers who say that happiness has been rising after all (Veenhoven and Hagerty, 2003; Stevenson and Wolfers, 2008; Deaton, 2008). That controversy is not the subject of this chapter. We shall content ourselves with the simple fact that the large rise in GDP in the last 50 years has not been matched by a proportionate rise in subjective wellbeing.

For critics of the free market, this is a vindication of their belief that capitalism has come to the end of its road. Although Easterlin never claimed that people would be happier in a 'steady-state' (i.e. zero-growth) economy than in a flourishing free market, others have made this claim for him. These 'growth sceptics' (Ben-Ami, 2010) might grudgingly admit that two centuries of increasing prosperity have improved living standards to an unprecedented degree. They might even be coaxed into conceding that life has been better in the capitalist West than in the workers' paradises of the USSR. But, they insist, flatlining happiness shows that the benefits of growth have finally been wrung dry and that a different economic system is required if the people are to reach euphoria.

The 'non-relationship' between happiness and equality

Having made the doubtful assumption that economic stagnation does not make people miserable, the growth sceptics have further hypothesised that equalising incomes will achieve what raising incomes apparently cannot. It has been suggested that people living in 'more equal' societies are happier than those who live in countries where the gap between rich and poor is wider. If so, it would mean that wealth redistribution is more important than wealth creation. By a happy coincidence, that is exactly what those who make such claims have always believed.

The idea that egalitarian societies enjoy higher life satisfaction scores is more widely held by political commentators and left-wing activists than by those who are familiar with the academic literature. The *Guardian* columnist Polly Toynbee insists that 'every model shows that the most unequal societies are the least happy'. This is simply untrue. Even the book Toynbee cites as supporting evidence – *The Spirit Level* – never explicitly states that more equal societies score higher in surveys of happiness and wellbeing.

The take-home message of *The Spirit Level* certainly seems to be that 'more equal societies are happier', but these are words that have been put in the mouths of its authors Richard Wilkinson and Kate Pickett, albeit without much of a struggle from the two social epidemiologists. When pressed on this question, they have conceded that 'there is no relation between inequality and WVS [World Values Survey] measures of happiness' (Wilkinson and Pickett, 2010), although they have complained that self-reported evidence is 'notoriously unreliable'.

Unreliable it may be, but not so unreliable as to prevent Wilkinson and Pickett from using the self-reported happiness statistics in *The Spirit Level*'s opening pages to show that 'happiness levels fail to rise further as rich countries get still richer' (ibid.: 8).[2] With this nod of the head to the Easterlin paradox, they spend the rest of the book making the case that although economic growth has reached the limits of utility, reducing income inequality will improve a nation's performance in everything from infant mortality to the amount of rubbish that is recycled.

That these improvements will lead to greater happiness is so strongly implied that Toynbee can be forgiven for her error. But while the book includes dozens of graphs showing how nations perform across various criteria, the happiness data are never put to the same test. Although the happiness surveys are considered reliable enough to challenge the conventional belief that higher incomes lead to greater happiness, the hypothesis that greater income equality leads to greater happiness is never required to meet the same burden of proof. There is a good reason for that. Figure 10 shows the total lack of correlation between income inequality and happiness in the world's richest countries.

Self-described egalitarians are eager to cite the straight line of subjective wellbeing since 1965 as damning proof that economic growth is useless, but they seldom mention that inequality has also had no observable effect on happiness in the last 50 years. In light of Easterlin's work, no test could be more obvious than to compare rates of inequality with levels of happiness over time, but remarkably few social scientists have bothered to do so. Arthur C. Brooks is a rare exception (Brooks, 2007). By studying the results of America's General Social Survey (GSS), he found a conspicuous lack of association between the two variables:

---

2   Other self-reported measures such as trust and child wellbeing are also included in *The Spirit Level*.

Figure 10 **Feel 'very happy' or 'quite happy'**

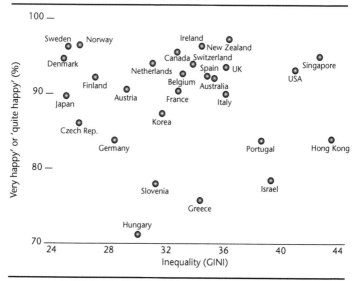

If the egalitarians are right, then average happiness levels should be falling. But they aren't. The GSS shows that in 1972, 30 percent of the population said that they were 'very happy' with their lives; in 1982, 31 percent; in 1993, 32 percent; in 2004, 31 percent. In other words, no significant change in reported happiness occurred – even as income inequality increased by nearly half. Happiness levels have certainly shown some fluctuations over the last three decades, but income inequality explains none of them.

Figure 11 shows inequality charted against levels of happiness in the USA since 1965 (Johns and Ormerod, 2007: 40). Again, the obvious lack of association supports the view that inequality has little or no impact on happiness.

Measures of happiness are inevitably based on subjective data

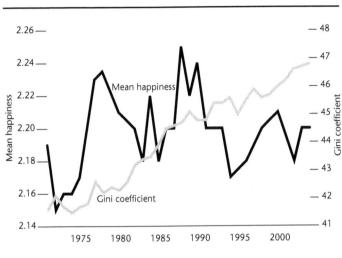

Figure 11 **Mean happiness and income inequality (as measured by the Gini coefficient) in the USA, 1971–2004**

and it has long been accepted that human beings become accustomed to a higher standard of living and move their aspirations upwards. This pattern of constantly improving living standards is gloomily referred to as the 'hedonic treadmill'. The search for a more objective measure of wellbeing led some researchers to view the revealed preference of suicide as a proxy for unhappiness (Koivumaa-Honkanen et al., 2003; Daly and Wilson, 2008).

The scientific literature shows that there is no positive association between inequality and suicide (Mellor and Milyo, 2001; Rodríguez, 2005; Minoiu and Rodríguez, 2008). As Figure 12 shows, when rich nations are compared, the correlation runs in the opposite direction. Suicide rates tend to be lower where inequality is greater – a negative association that is accepted even

Figure 12 **Suicide rate per 100,000**

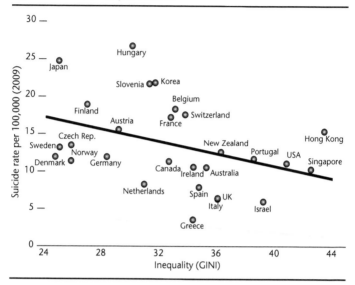

in *The Spirit Level* (Wilkinson and Pickett, 2009: 175): the authors do, however, insist that a higher suicide rate is a trade-off for a lower homicide rate, but this is not an argument that stands up against the facts (Snowdon, 2010: 82).

Whether one compares 'more equal' countries with 'less equal' countries, or whether one studies each country over time, the national mood remains stubbornly indifferent to levels of income inequality. This holds true whether one looks at happiness, subjective wellbeing, life satisfaction or proxies for all three.

The academic literature on happiness and inequality

Comparing crude data between whole countries is a blunt

instrument, but more sophisticated attempts to test whether inequality affects happiness have not produced compelling evidence. Perhaps the most thought-provoking of these was the study by Alesina et al. (2004), which found that happiness was sometimes affected by inequality, but was principally dependent on social attitudes rather than inequality per se, a conclusion echoed by Biancotti and D'Alessio (2008), Hopkins (2008) and Bjørnskov et al. (2010). While it might be expected that the rich would be less troubled by inequality than the poor, this was not necessarily the case. Alesina et al. found low-income Europeans to be averse to inequality, while low-income Americans were 'totally unaffected'. Rich Americans were often more averse to inequality than their poorer compatriots, while left-wingers were more sensitive to changes in wealth distribution on both sides of the Atlantic.

Alesina et al. explained the paradox of American tolerance to inequality, despite a wealth gap that dwarfs most European countries, by reference to the prevailing belief that wealth is the product of hard work and merit – a view that is widely shared in Europe only by the rich. In contrast to Europeans, Americans are inclined to view inequality as justified and wealth redistribution as unfair. Americans have greater faith in social mobility, with the poor expecting to move up the ladder and the rich fearing they might move down. Alesina et al. found that 60 per cent of Europeans believed the poor were trapped in poverty, while only 30 per cent of Americans felt the same way. When asked whether the poor were lazy, the percentages were exactly reversed.

Regardless of whether these beliefs are grounded in reality, the study showed that perceptions of fairness and social mobility are more important than inequality itself. Some people are made less happy by inequality while others rather like it. A greater proportion is largely indifferent. This may be because they are unaware of the scale of inequality in their country or because they do not view inequality as inherently unfair. Whatever the individual reaction may be, there is no suggestion that either Americans or Europeans are so outraged by inequality that this one economic variable could drag down the happiness of the entire nation.

Evidence that inequality is directly related to lower levels of national happiness is scant indeed. Helliwell (2003) tentatively concluded that levels of wellbeing were higher when income was more evenly distributed, and Fischer (2009) found that life satisfaction scores were negatively associated with post-tax income inequality. Graham and Felton (2005) found mixed evidence of inequality affecting happiness in Latin America.

Ott (2005) and Clark (2003), on the other hand, found that happiness was positively associated with income inequality, with the latter concluding that 'individuals appear to be inequality-loving rather than inequality-averse' (pp. 9–10). An earlier study by Tomes (1986) came to a similar conclusion and, in a study of 119 nations, Berg and Veenhoven (2010) found that inequality did not have a negative effect on happiness. After controlling for absolute income, Berg and Veenhoven actually reported a possible beneficial effect:

> In the present day world, there is little relation between income inequality in nations and average happiness of citizens. Controlling for wealth, a slightly positive correlation emerges. There is no clear level of income inequality beyond which happiness declines. Income inequality is not correlated with inequality in happiness after controlling for wealth. Although income inequality

might have downsides, these are apparently outweighed by
the positive aspects of income inequality.

The majority of studies have found that inequality does not
have a significant effect on happiness in either direction. It would
be tedious to list them all, but to give a few examples, Luttmer
(2004) and Bjørnskov et al. (2010) found that inequality had
no effect on happiness; Fahey and Smyth (2004) found it had
no effect on life satisfaction; Senik (2002) found no evidence of
an effect on happiness in Russia; Schwarze and Härpfer (2003)
found no evidence that reducing inequality improved wellbeing
in Germany; Veenhoven (1996) found no correlation between
income inequality and 'happy life-expectancy'; and Helliwell and
Huang's study of 75 countries (2006) found no effect from income
inequality on subjective wellbeing.

There is, in short, a vanishingly small amount of evidence
to support the proposition that inequality has a negative effect
on the happiness of societies. Inequality may affect different
people in different ways, depending on the country they live in,
their political views and their own income. These effects can be
positive, negative or non-existent, but they have little or no influence on the wellbeing of society as a whole.

In their review of the literature, Clark and Senik (2010)
concluded that empirical work has 'struggled to establish an
unambiguous relationship between ex post income inequality
and happiness'. A similar paper by Hopkins (2008) noted that
'in briefly surveying the recent theoretical literature, it became
clear that there are plausible models of relative concerns where
inequality is bad, where it is good and where different forms of
inequality can have opposite effects'.

For the libertarian commentator Will Wilkinson, the happiness literature is a vindication of the American economic model: 'The data show that neither higher rates of government redistribution nor lower levels of income inequality make us happier, whereas high levels of economic freedom and high average incomes are among the strongest correlates of subjective well-being' (Wilkinson, 2007: 1).

Commentators on the left have little ammunition with which to shoot down this argument. Even Richard Layard, an early adopter of the inequality/happiness hypothesis (Layard, 1980), accepts that 'there is as yet no clear evidence to show that inequality as such affects the happiness of individuals in a community' (Layard, 2005; 52). In his book *Happiness: Lessons from a new science*, he conceded that: 'The assumption used to be that people dislike inequality. But increasing evidence finds that some groups (those who are mobile or feel they are mobile) actually like it.'

Having accepted that inequality has little or no effect on happiness, Layard argues instead that an extra dollar earned gives more happiness to the poor than to the rich. This may be true, but while Layard cites this as an argument for income redistribution, it is really only an argument for making the poor richer, and it is far from certain that the poor would get richer faster in a steady-state egalitarian system than in a growing free market.

Happiness and relative income

With a mountain of research refuting the theory, why do so many people continue to believe that – to quote the London Equality Group – 'more equal societies are happier'? In part, this can be explained by the sometimes accidental misrepresentation of the academic literature in the popular press, but it is also the result of pundits confusing 'income inequality' with 'relative income'. It is an understandable confusion. The two concepts seem interchangeable, but relative income is not income inequality, as Clark and Senik (2010) point out: 'The two notions are of course different, as income comparisons refer to the specific income gap between individual income and the income of some relevant others, whereas income inequality refers to the entire distribution of income in society.'

This distinction may seem obvious to happiness scholars like Clark and Senik, but the two concepts have merged into one in the popular literature. Simply put, relative income is the difference between you and your neighbour, your friends and your family. Income inequality is the difference between the richest and poorest people in the country. Put still more simply, relative income involves jealous glances over the garden fence while income inequality requires envy of the distant rich.

The majority of studies into the effects of relative income have concluded that people's happiness is indeed affected by the income of those around them (Weisbach, 2008). The magnitude of the effect is open to question. Some studies have estimated that an extra dollar earned by one's neighbour has the same effect on happiness as ten to thirty cents lost personally (Layard, 2005: 46, 252). At the top end of these projections, both Ferrer-i-Carbonell (2005) and Luttmer (2004) calculated that an extra dollar earned by one's neighbour has about the same impact on happiness as a dollar lost by oneself.

The income of friends and neighbours affects happiness, in part, because it affects aspirations. As Stutzer (2004) has argued, wellbeing depends on the gap between earnings and aspirations.

When members of our reference group earn more and acquire new possessions, they show us that the standard of living we once thought was reserved for the rich is now within reach of people like ourselves.

That is part of it. The other part is straightforward 'status anxiety'. Perhaps the most famous behavioural experiment in this field involved students at the Harvard School of Public Health answering questions about relative and absolute income. Asked whether they would prefer to earn $50,000 when others earned half as much, or $100,000 when others earned twice as much, around half of them said they would take the lower wage over the lower status (Solnick and Hemenway, 1998).

This striking finding has been widely cited as proof of the overwhelming importance of relative income in modern society. It features prominently in Robert H. Frank's *Luxury Fever* as well as in *Happiness* and *The Spirit Level*. In the latter, it is cited as proof that 'people's desire for more income is really a desire for higher status' (Wilkinson and Pickett, 2009: 225).

This is a far-reaching conclusion to draw from such slim evidence. Since most of the respondents were students, few would have earned even $50,000 in real life and the questionnaire might have seemed a hypothetical test of morals. Those opting for the lower figure may have been expressing a distaste for materialism. Tellingly, members of staff were less likely to express a preference for sacrificing money for status.

A subsequent study by the same researchers produced some interesting results. When the survey turned to non-financial concerns, 18 per cent of students claimed to be in favour of having two 'unpleasant dental procedures' rather than just one, so long as other people had to endure four visits to the dentist instead of none. Thirteen per cent said they would accept a higher infant mortality rate rather than see other countries have fewer babies die: these, I repeat, were students of *public health*. When given the option of being ill for six days while others were sick for two days, 11 per cent of respondents claimed a preference for being ill for nine days so long as others were sick for twelve days. The same percentage said they would rather have their cars broken into more often and suffer worse air pollution so long as crime and pollution were even worse for other people (Solnick and Hemenway, 2005).

A worldly interpretation of these results would be that a significant minority of respondents were not taking the experiment altogether seriously, or did not understand the questions, or else had a profoundly strange outlook on life. Whatever the truth, it is clear that the battle for status involves much more than income. If people are prepared to undergo avoidable root canal surgery to move up a perceived pecking order, it is reasonable to assume they will compete over almost anything. While relative income does matter, all sorts of other relative values matter just as much. By focusing so relentlessly on money, the self-proclaimed egalitarians ignore the innate human desire for respect and status that would be no less powerful if material pleasures did not exist.

Can we deal with 'income envy' anyway?

Even if we make the false assumption that income envy is one of the main determinants of unhappiness in modern society, what is to be done? The significant thing about relative income, as the theorists never fail to mention, is not the possessions it affords, but the status it confers. It is not the size of the differential which feeds status competition so much as the fact that a differential exists. Relative income envy is inevitable whenever incomes vary, and the psychological effects of relative income cannot be alleviated: they either exist or they do not. Merely *reducing* the gap will not help because status can be conferred by a single extra dollar. If relative income is a problem at all, it is one that can be solved only by making sure no one has more than anyone else.

Karl Marx gave us his take on relative income anxiety in *Wage, Labour and Capital* (1847): 'A house may be large or small; as long as the neighbouring houses are likewise small, it satisfies all social requirement for a residence. But let there arise next to the little house a palace, and the little house shrinks to a hut.'

Like so many of Marx's ideas, this makes more sense in theory than in practice. In the real world, no one builds a palace in a street of small houses. Whether you are rich or poor, your neighbour's house is likely to be similar in size, if not identical, to your own. And it is your neighbour, not some distant billionaire, who can affect your wellbeing. As Alain de Botton says in *Status Anxiety*: 'We envy only those whom we feel ourselves to be like; we envy only members of our reference group' (2004: 47).

Whether we reside on Millionaire's Avenue or Skid Row, our reference group consists of people who are similar to ourselves. If positional concerns were paramount, we would expect the rich to move into poorer neighbourhoods to get the full benefit of their relative wealth! In reality, like the rest of us, they tend to live among those who have comparable incomes. Consequently, there tends to be very little income inequality on any given street. Indeed, many parts of Britain could benefit from a little less equality and a little more income. Conversely, in many farming villages, significant income inequality exists between landowners, tenant farmers, labourers and the rural poor while they manage to attain a level of social harmony of which people living in more egalitarian tower blocks could only dream.

Inequalities are neither severe nor damaging between friends and neighbours, and it is they who are the relevant reference group. Even if we view the effect of 'over-the-garden-fence' inequality as a suitable case for treatment, traditional policies of wealth redistribution are unlikely to be effective because, as Niemietz (2011: 102) points out, neighbours are generally in the same tax bracket.

Concerns about relative income have an effect on aspirations, and therefore on happiness, but these concerns are just as prevalent in 'more equal' countries as they are in 'less equal' countries (unless those 'more equal' countries practise doctrinally pure communism). Conflating status competition between individuals with income inequality at the national level is a red herring in this discussion.

Attitudes to inequality

In 2007, the Institute for Social and Economic Research sought an answer to the question of why 'most people appear to accept widespread social and economic inequalities' in the UK (Pahl et al., 2007). Based on survey results, they found that Britons were not greatly troubled by the higher incomes of others, regardless of whether these others were distant or close:

> We find that, in many ways, social comparisons are still
> narrow and knowledge of the true extent of inequality is still
> limited. What comparisons people do make appear to be
> based on lifestyle and consumption. Hence, they are neither

resentful of the super-rich, nor of others closer to themselves who have done better in life. However, they are very aware of their advantages compared with less fortunate members of society.

We do not, by and large, compare ourselves with 'the distant rich', as J. K. Galbraith called them, and yet it is the distant rich who preoccupy the minds of the inequality theorists. Contrary to all evidence, Wilkinson and Pickett insist that: 'By comparison with the rich and famous, the rest of us appear second-rate and inferior ... the consumption of the rich reduces everyone else's satisfaction with what they have, by showing it up as inferior' (2009: 222).

Oliver James strikes a similar chord in his anti-consumerist polemic *Affluenza*: 'Once, we used to keep up with the Joneses who lived in our street. Now, thanks largely to TV, it's the Beckhams' (2007: 42).

Let us briefly entertain the idea that Oliver James might be correct and that status anxieties do not jump over the garden fence but seep into our homes via the television aerial. Leaving aside the fact that 'more equal' countries such as Sweden have plenty of high-profile billionaires and footballers of their own, we must ask whether the 'problem' of rich people appearing on television is one that has a practical solution.

The question, again, is what can be done? Having accepted that the effects of relative income can be addressed only by making all incomes the same, the government might enforce total wage parity in a given neighbourhood. This, however, would still leave citizens susceptible to happiness-impeding images of their more prosperous countrymen on the television. The government might then bring about income equality across the land, but, even then, the super-rich of other countries would remain on screen. Since the government cannot force other countries to go down the same egalitarian path, the only effective way of stopping people feeling 'second-rate and inferior' would be to seize control of the media and ban foreign television. In other words, a society that wishes to maximise its happiness by minimising anxieties over relative income must introduce total wage parity and cut itself off from the outside world. This is not a system that has improved life satisfaction scores in countries where it has been tried.

Inequality theorists would criticise this as a 'reductio ad North Korea' argument. They would protest that they are not proposing income equality in the literal sense. Instead, they are calling for countries to be 'more equal', an oxymoron that comes straight out of Orwell's *Animal Farm*. But the scenario I present is not intended to be facetious. Rather, it is the only logical solution to the problems that trouble the inequality theorists. In this instance, it really is an all-or-nothing situation. The effect of relative income anxiety can be alleviated only by stopping incomes being relative, and our (supposedly) self-harming desire to keep up with 'the Beckhams' on TV can be cured only by getting rid of the Beckhams or by getting rid of TV.

Having indulged Oliver James in his belief that we judge ourselves by the standards of millionaire footballers, let us return to the happiness studies, which show nothing of the sort. Even if rich people being on television was a proxy for inequality – and it isn't – the evidence does not support the view that they are hazardous to happiness. What the evidence actually shows is that the income of friends, family and neighbours is *one of the factors* that have *some effect* on personal happiness for *some people*.

Contrary to James et al., it is the Joneses who remain our reference group and, unsurprisingly, it is the people we socialise with most often who have the greatest impact on our aspirations and wellbeing. Luttmer (2004), for example, found that 'the effect of neighbours' earnings is significantly stronger for those who socialize more frequently with neighbours but not for those who socialize more frequently with relatives, friends outside the neighbourhood, or people they work with'.

Blanchflower and Oswald's nine-word conclusion is as succinct and accurate an assessment of the evidence as one could hope to find: 'Money buys happiness. People care also about relative income.'

Of the two, money is the most important. Bartolini et al. (2008), for example, stress that 'absolute income is the main positive contributor to happiness'. This simple truth is not reflected in some of the popular literature which goes far beyond the evidence by suggesting that greater wealth does *not* make us happier and that possessions are desired for no other reason than to assert one's status. This leads to sweeping statements such as this from *The Spirit Level*: 'Instead of a better society, *the only thing* almost everyone strives for is to better their own position – as individuals – within the existing society' (Wilkinson and Pickett, 2009: 4; my emphasis).

In fact, happiness studies have been effective in showing that we strive for all sorts of things and that few of them have anything to do with our own money, let alone other people's. Belief in God (Helliwell, 2004), good government (Helliwell and Huang, 2006), personal freedom (Veenhoven, 2000a, 2000b), economic freedom (Ott, 2005) and social capital (Luttmer, 2004) have all been shown to improve happiness. Unemployment (Clark and Oswald, 1994),

Figure 13 **'Most people can be trusted'**

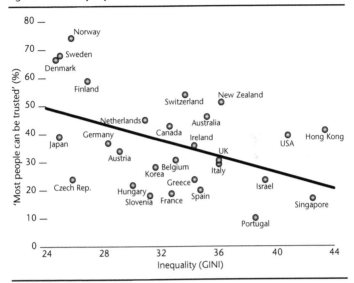

chronic illness and divorce (Di Tella and MacCulloch, 2008) have all been shown to cause unhappiness. The cash equivalent of a lasting marriage has been tentatively estimated at $100,000 a year while unemployment costs the individual the equivalent of $60,000 a year in happiness (Blanchflower and Oswald, 2004).

Based on these observations, we might reasonably expect the happiest nations to be those which have large numbers of religious believers, a strong sense of community, low unemployment, low divorce rates and an open government which encourages personal and economic freedom. Do the 'more equal' nations fit this bill? In almost every case, the answer is 'no'.

Figures 13 and 14 show two measures of social capital: levels of self-reported trust and levels of involvement with community

Figure 14 **Membership of community groups**

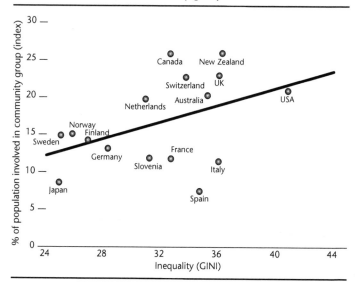

organizations (sports clubs, charities, religious groups and arts groups). Figure 15 shows the Heritage Foundation's measure of economic freedom. Figure 16 shows the proportion of the population who agree with the statement 'God is very important in my life' and Figures 17 and 18 show two factors that negatively affect happiness: unemployment and divorce.

The Scandinavian nations all perform unusually well on the measure of trust, but this does not seem to be the result of greater income equality since the overall correlation is weak and many of the 'less equal' countries have high levels of trust. There is a similarly weak correlation between inequality and community involvement, but in this instance the data show that the 'less equal' countries perform better. There are stronger correlations

Figure 15 **Economic freedom (Heritage Foundation 2011)**

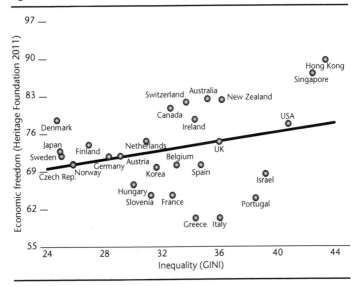

Figure 16 **'God is very important in my life' (%)**

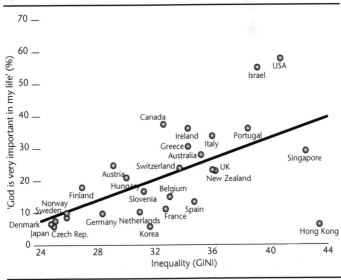

Figure 17 **Average unemployment, 1995–2005 (%)**

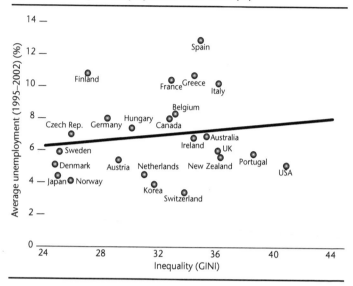

Figure 18 **Percentage of marriages ending in divorce**

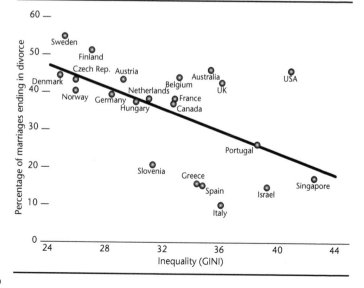

showing that people in 'less equal' countries are less likely to be divorced and are more likely to be religious, although it is difficult to see a causal pathway for either. Finally, there is little indication that 'more equal' countries enjoy greater economic freedom or less unemployment.

In summary, there is no empirical evidence that people in more egalitarian countries enjoy happier lives, nor is there any credible reason to think they should. Scholars of happiness have identified many factors which improve life satisfaction scores but income equality is not one of them. Furthermore, since none of the factors which *have* been shown to boost happiness is more abundant in the 'more equal' nations, it is unlikely that those societies would be happier even by chance.

Devoid of support in the academic literature, the myth that 'more equal' countries are happier is the creation of a political faction Niemietz (2011) terms *über-relativists*, who have taken the modest observation that some people raise their aspirations in line with people they know as evidence that anxiety about income inequality is the main determinant of happiness in the Western world. Having taken this position, it makes sense to them that countries with the lowest levels of income inequality should be the happiest. The *über-relativists* have to navigate so many obstacles of logic to arrive at this position that the mere fact that 'more equal' societies are *not* happier by any empirical measure is not enough to make them turn back.

Insofar as 'happiness studies' is a 'new science' at all, it is not one that offers sustenance to those who pursue an egalitarian agenda. If one is looking for a sound basis for a happier life, one might heed the words of Diener and Biswas-Diener (2009), who conclude: 'Thus: our advice is to avoid poverty, live in a rich country, and focus on goals other than material wealth.' This might be stating the obvious, but happiness research rarely does otherwise.

References

Alesina, A., R. DiTella and R. MacCulloch (2004), 'Happiness and inequality: are Europeans and Americans different?', *Journal of Public Economics*, 88(9/10): 2009–42.

Bartolini, S. et al. (2008), 'Did the decline in social capital depress Americans' happiness?', Quaderni del Dipartimento di Economia Politica, Università degli Studi di Siena, no. 540.

Ben-Ami, D. (2010), *Ferraris for All*, Bristol: Policy Press.

Berg, M. and R. Veenhoven (2010), 'Income inequality and happiness in 119 nations', in B. Greve (ed.), *Social Policy and Happiness in Europe*, Cheltenham: Edward Elgar, pp. 174–94.

Biancotti, C. and G. D'Alessio (2008), 'Values, inequality and happiness', Bank of Italy Working Paper no. 669.

Bjørnskov, C. et al. (2010), 'On the relation between income inequality and happiness: do fairness perceptions matter?', Discussion Paper Series no. 495, University of Heidelberg.

Blanchflower, D. and A. Oswald (2004), 'Well-being over time in Britain and the USA', *Journal of Public Economics*, 88: 1359–86.

Brooks, A. C. (2007), 'What really buys happiness', *City Journal*, Summer.

Burkett, J. (2006), 'How much will people pay for status', *American Economist*, 50(1): 80–88.

Clark, A. (2003), 'Inequality-aversion and income mobility: a direct test', DELTA Discussion Paper no. 2003–11.

Clark, A. and A. Oswald (1994), 'Unhappiness and unemployment', *Economic Journal*, 104: 648–59.

Clark, A. and C. Senik (2010), 'Who compares to whom? The anatomy of income comparisons in Europe', *Economic Journal*, 120: 573–94.

Daly, M. and D. Wilson (2008), 'Happiness, unhappiness, and suicide: an empirical assessment', Working Paper 2008–19, Federal Reserve Bank of San Francisco, August.

De Botton, A. (2004), *Status Anxiety*, London: Hamish Hamilton.

Deaton, A. (2008), 'Income, health and wellbeing around the world: evidence from the Gallup World Poll', *Journal of Economic Perspectives*, 22(2): 53–72.

Di Tella, R. and R. MacCulloch (2008), 'Gross national happiness as an answer to the Easterlin Paradox?', *Journal of Development Economics*, 86(1): 22–42.

Diener, E. and R. Biswas-Diener (2009), 'Will money increase subjective well-being?', *Social Indicators Research*, 37: 119–54.

Fahey, A. L. and E. Smyth (2004), 'The link between subjective well-being and objective conditions in European societies', in W. Arts and L. Halman (eds), *European Values at the Turn of the Millennium*, Brill, pp. 57–80.

Ferrer-i-Carbonell, A. (2005), 'Income and well-being: an empirical analysis of the comparison income effect', *Journal of Public Economics*, 89: 997–1019.

Fischer, J. A. (2009), 'The welfare effects of social mobility', OECD Social, Employment and Migration Working Papers no. 93, Paris: OECD Publishing.

Graham, C. and A. Felton (2005), 'Does inequality matter to individual welfare? An initial exploration based on happiness surveys from Latin America', CSED Working Paper no. 38.

Helliwell, J. (2003), 'How's life? Combining individual and national variables to explain subjective well-being', *Economic Modelling*, 20: 331–60.

Helliwell, J. (2004), 'Well-being and social capital: does suicide pose a puzzle?', National Bureau of Economic Research Working Paper 10896.

Helliwell, J. and H. Huang (2006), 'How's your government? International evidence linking good government and well-being', NBER Working Paper no. 11988, January.

Hopkins, E. (2008), 'Inequality, happiness and relative concerns: what actually is their relationship?', *Journal of Economic Inequality*, 6(4): 351–72.

James, O. (2007), *Affluenza*, London: Vermilion.

Johns, H. and P. Ormerod (2007), *Happiness, Economics and Public Policy*, London: Institute of Economic Affairs.

Koivumaa-Honkanen, H. et al. (2003), 'Self-reported happiness in life and suicide in ensuing 20 years', *Social Psychiatry and Psychiatric Epidemiology*, 38(5): 244–8.

Layard, R. (1980), 'Human satisfactions and public policy', *Economic Journal*, 90(360): 737–50.

Layard, R. (2005), *Happiness: Lessons from a new science*, London: Penguin.

Layard, R., G. Mayraz and S. Nickell (2009), 'Does relative income matter? Are the critics right?', CEP Discussion Paper no. 918, March.

Luttmer, E. (2004), 'Neighbors as negatives: relative earnings and well-being', KSG Faculty Research Working Paper Series RWP04–029.

Mellor, J. M. and J. Milyo (2001), 'Re-examining the ecological association between income inequality and health', *Journal of Health Politics Policy and Law*, 26: 487–522.

Minoiu, C. and A. Rodríguez (2008), 'The effect of public spending on suicide: evidence from U.S. state data', *Journal of Socio-Economics*, 37: 237–61.

Niemietz, K. (2011), *A New Understanding of Poverty*, London: Institute of Economic Affairs.

Ott, J. (2005), 'Level and inequality of happiness in nations: does greater happiness of a greater number imply greater inequality in happiness?', *Journal of Happiness Studies*, 6(4): 397–420.

Pahl, R., D. Rose and L. Spencer (2007), 'Inequality and quiescence: a continuing conundrum', Institute for Social and Economic Research Working Paper 2007–22.

Rodríguez, A. (2005), 'Income inequality, unemployment and suicide: a panel data analysis of 15 European countries', *Applied Economics*, 37: 439–451.

Schwarze, J. and M. Härpfer (2003), 'Are people inequality averse, and do they prefer redistribution by the state?', Discussion Paper no. 974, Institute for the Study of Labour, December.

Senik, C. (2002), 'When information dominates comparison: a panel data analysis using Russian subjective panel data', William Davidson Institute Working Paper Series 495, University of Michigan.

Snowdon, C. (2010), *The Spirit Level Delusion*, London: Little Dice.

Solnick, S. and D. Hemenway (1998), 'Is more always better?: a survey on positional concerns', *Journal of Economic Behavior and Organization*, 37: 373–83.

Solnick, S. and D. Hemenway (2005), 'Are positional concerns stronger in some domains than in others?', *American Economic Review*, 95(2): 147–51.

Stevenson, B. and J. Wolfers (2008), 'Economic growth and subjective well-being: reassessing the Easterlin Paradox', NBER Working Paper no. 14282.

Stutzer, A. (2004), 'The role of income aspirations in individual happiness', *Journal of Economic Behavior and Organization*, 54(1): 89–109.

Tomes, N. (1986), 'Income distribution, happiness and satisfaction: a direct test of the interdependent preferences model', *Journal of Economic Psychology*, 7: 425–46.

Toynbee, P. (2010), 'An unhappiness index is more David Cameron's style', *Guardian*, 16 November.

Veenhoven, R. (1996), 'Happy life-expectancy: a comprehensive measure of quality-of-life in nations', *Social Indicators Research*, 39: 1–58.

Veenhoven, R. (2000a), 'Freedom and happiness', in E. Diener and E. M. Suh (eds), *Culture and Subjective Wellbeing*, MIT Press.

Veenhoven, R. (2000b), 'Wellbeing in the welfare state', *Journal of Comparative Policy Analysis*, 2: 91–125.

Veenhoven, R. and M. R. Hagerty (2003), 'Wealth and happiness revisited: growing wealth of nations does go with greater happiness', *Social Indicators Research*, 64: 1–27.

Verme, P. (2011), 'Life satisfaction and income inequality', *Review of Income and Wealth*, 57(1): 111–27.

Weisbach, D. (2008), 'What does happiness research tell us about taxation?', *Journal of Legal Studies*, 37(S2): 293–324.

Wilkinson, R. and K. Pickett (2009), *The Spirit Level*, London: Allen Lane.

Wilkinson, R. and K. Pickett (2010), 'Professors Richard Wilkinson and Kate Pickett, authors of *The Spirit Level*, reply to critics', http://equalityportal.net/wp-content/uploads/group-documents/4/1289149154-response-to-snowdon.pdf.

Wilkinson, W. (2007), *In Pursuit of Happiness Research. Is It Reliable? What Does it Imply for Policy?*, Policy Analysis No. 590, Washington D.C.: Cato Institute.

PART TWO: HAPPINESS AND GOVERNMENT INTERVENTION

5 WELLBEING AT WORK: ANY LESSONS?
J. R. Shackleton

Paid work is a very important aspect of the lives of most adults. It provides income on which they depend for a decent living standard in a monetised economy. But it also offers a structure to their daily lives, provides social contact and builds personal identities and self-esteem (OECD, 2008). It is unlikely to diminish in importance any time soon, as more of us now expect to extend employment well beyond the early to mid-sixties which came to mark 'normal' retirement age over the last 30 years. So it is not surprising that the current upsurge of interest in the economics and psychology of happiness and wellbeing attaches a great deal of significance to the world of work.

Over the last fifteen years, advances in statistical and econometric techniques, exponential increases in cheap computing power, and the wide availability of large-scale surveys using indicators of wellbeing have led to a burgeoning academic literature. In addition to the intrinsic interest of the subject, there is also the intriguing argument that improvements in wellbeing may be translated into higher commitment to the job, higher productivity and improved economic performance.

This has fuelled a lively policy debate in which the ever-growing 'human resources' (HR) profession has been prominent. The Chartered Institute of Personnel and Development notes the relevance of findings about wellbeing at work to issues such as absenteeism, the high level of incapacity benefit claims and the promotion of mental health. It is one of many bodies stressing the importance of 'creating an environment to promote a state of contentment which allows an employee to flourish and achieve their full potential for the benefit of themselves and their organisation' (CIPD, 2007: 4). This leads some commentators (for instance, Brinkley et al., 2010) to argue for increased government regulation to promote this objective.

This chapter outlines the theoretical background, methodology and findings of the recent academic literature. There is much of interest in this literature for economists. The chapter's conclusions, however, question the orthodoxy that supports sometimes costly changes in personnel practices by employers or regulatory interventions by government.

Objective and subjective measures of wellbeing at work

Looking purely at directly observable measures, the conditions under which most people work in this country have never been better. Crafts (2007) reports on long-run improvements in living standards over the course of the twentieth century, citing increased real earnings, improved health, greater life expectancy and reduced poverty. Work is less dangerous and less tiring[1] and, with higher incomes, people also have more choice over occupations, hours worked and location. Work involves greater use of skills and education, offers more variety and less repetition, and

---

1　Partly as a result of legislation but probably more importantly as a result of firms using new technologies, and producing goods and services which demand less physical and manual labour to produce, as a consequence of the switch from manufacturing and extraction towards services.

gives more opportunities for interaction with fellow workers and customers or clients. Although no job is ever wholly secure, unwanted levels of casual employment (such as those that used to prevail in the docks) are largely a thing of the past.

The average 'quality' of jobs, measured by this type of objective indicator, has surely risen dramatically over the last century. And these jobs are available to a wider range of the population, with women now accounting for almost 50 per cent of the workforce.[2]

But most of the focus in the literature is on states of mind rather than objective aspects of the work environment. Subjective wellbeing at work comprises a number of elements – physical and mental health, social interaction and satisfaction with a range of job attributes. Psychologists (for example, Robertson and Cooper, 2011) distinguish between two facets of personal wellbeing deriving from work – 'hedonic', meaning subjective pleasure, happiness and positive feelings, and 'eudaimonic', involving a sense of purpose, personal growth and the conviction that one has respect and a place in society.

The research flowing from this focuses on using survey data to help identify factors (including both personal attributes and job

2   There may be fluctuations in job quality over shorter periods. There is some evidence (Green, 2004; Brown et al., 2006) to suggest that work intensity rose in the 1990s in the UK as a result of closer monitoring facilitated by changes in work organisation and computer technology; this was regarded as oppressive by some groups of workers. Intensity did not, however, continue to increase into the new century and between 1998 and 2004 there appears to have been a significant improvement in many aspects of job quality, including training, employment security and the degree of influence individuals had over their work (Michie et al., 2008). Moreover, Green (2011) and Waldfogel (2011), reviewing a slightly longer period, argue that, over the term of the last government, pay rose, hours of work fell and new employment 'rights' (such as enhanced parental leave) were made available, thus further improving the directly observable quality of people's work experience.

characteristics) which are strongly associated with indicators of psychological wellbeing.

Surveys typically use questions based on Likert scales (for example, respondents may be asked to rate job satisfaction on a five-point scale ranging from 'very satisfied' to 'very dissatisfied'). Putting numbers to these answers enables quick comparisons between average scores for different occupations, genders, age groups and even (as we shall see later) countries. In more sophisticated analysis of large-scale data sets, the separate effects of a wide range of explanatory variables can be estimated.

Studies of this kind have identified a number of work characteristics which are claimed to have a statistically significant influence on job satisfaction and broader indicators of wellbeing at work (European Foundation for the Improvement of Living and Working Conditions, 2007b; Michie et al., 2008). Positives include 'hedonic' factors such as above-average pay, the size of the workplace (smaller workplaces being preferred), having a secure job, individual control over the pace of work, and the opportunity to work at home; 'eudaimonic' factors include the opportunity to use a range of skills and work which is seen as socially useful.[3] Negatives include tight deadlines, close monitoring and performance targets.

These findings have led some academics (for example, Cooper and Dewe, 2009; Robertson and Cooper, 2011) to extol 'good jobs' and 'good work'[4] embodying the positive characteristics noted above; by contrast, there are 'bad jobs' which are denigrated.

---

3   It is also notable that self-employment is associated with high levels of job satisfaction and wellbeing – despite typically lower average pay, longer hours of work and less security.

4   Is it a coincidence that the list of features of 'good jobs' seems to correspond fairly closely to the characteristics of typical academic posts? Academics are themselves no fans of tight deadlines, close monitoring and performance targets.

These poor-quality jobs are claimed to create stress (see Box overleaf) and may damage physical and/or mental health.

Research also shows, however, that after controlling for workplace characteristics, there are differences in job satisfaction and wellbeing which are associated with personal characteristics. Most obviously, in the UK at least, women consistently show higher levels of job satisfaction than men. Their preferences are also different: working in the public sector adding to job satisfaction for women, but not for men, for example. Ethnicity is a factor, with black employees less satisfied than white employees. Age is also relevant, with younger workers less satisfied than older ones (though the relationship is not straightforward). Graduates are less happy than non-graduates. Non-unionised workers appear to be happier than unionised workers. Place in the job hierarchy is also a factor, with managers more satisfied than other workers.[5]

In addition to these broad categories, it is also the case that people differ in their psychological wellbeing at work as a result

---

5   This mixture of workplace and personal characteristics as determinants of subjective job satisfaction has a counterpart in explanations of more objective indicators such as turnover rates and sickness absences – which may be considered as manifestations of *dis*satisfaction with jobs. Low turnover is associated with high relative pay, unionisation and the availability of training among workplace characteristics. At a personal level, men are more likely to quit for better-paid jobs than women, while higher-grade staff are more likely to move than lower-grade employees. As for sickness absence, analysis of UK Labour Force Survey data (Leaker, 2008) shows that, controlling for other factors, employees in workplaces with more than 500 employees are 34 per cent more likely to be absent than those in workplaces with fewer than 25 employees. Those working in the public sector are 22 per cent more likely to take sickness leave than those in the private sector. But personal characteristics – gender, ethnicity and age –have a significant impact as well. For instance, perhaps surprisingly, employees aged 16 to 24 are 32 per cent more likely to be absent than those aged 50 to 59 (women)/64 (men).

Stressed out?

The general morbidity of the working-age population has not increased, and numbers of work accidents have fallen considerably in the last 50 years. So people ought to be absent from work less often. The most common causes of all absence from work are colds, flu and backache, but the single biggest cause of long-term absence is stress. Longitudinal data from the British Household Panel Survey, using the General Health Questionnaire, show a sharp increase in incidence of self-reported stress in the 1990s, particularly for those working in the public sector. There is some evidence of a parallel increase in other European countries (European Foundation for the Improvement of Living and Working Conditions, 2007c).

Stress is an issue which creates a good deal of controversy. It is not easy to define: one author claims to have uncovered 650 different definitions. In the employment context it relates to individuals' feelings of being unable to cope with their workload. It is a psychological state of unease, but has physiological correlates such as high levels of cortisol in the body, and prolonged periods of stress can be a precipitating factor in cardiovascular and other serious illnesses. Stress at work may lead to erratic behaviour and poor performance. But what does it mean to say that stress at work has increased? Jones and Bright (2001) have argued that we should treat with some caution claims that people are suffering much higher levels of stress than they did in the past. They point out that the concept of stress was not clearly developed or widely discussed until recently. Certainly, when you consider the largely office-based occupations in central government, which report some of the highest levels of stress, it is difficult to see why such jobs are intrinsically more stressful than, say, coal mining, which occupied a substantial proportion of the workforce 50 years ago.

High levels of reported stress in a working environment have been seen in the literature to be associated with job content, the pace of work, interpersonal work relations, working hours, job security, control over workload, organisational culture, communications, and personal development opportunities. It is also known that non-manual workers are more likely than manual workers to report stress. Evidence from the Civil Service suggests that those higher up the hierarchy are less likely to suffer than those lower down. There are, however, some largely unexplained variations by occupation and, oddly, by region.

Work-related stress is, however, often very difficult to disentangle at an individual level from stress related to personal relationships and circumstances. One way of looking at stress at work is to see it as a conflict between emotions and the rationality of the work process. Changes in the work process lead to greater perceived stress, just as changes in personal relationships in private life are seen as stressful. It has been argued that the increase in reported stress in the UK public sector has been the result of a new managerial rationalism being applied to the work process, although changes in large parts of the public sector have sometimes been more superficial than has been claimed by critics.

The 'official' UK position on stress is that employers have a duty of care to employees which includes minimising work-related stress. The Health and Safety Executive (HSE) has published management standards which enjoin employers to consider such factors as the impact of workload and work patterns, the degree of control employees have over their work, management and colleague support, the need for a clear understanding of the individual's role, and the way in which change is managed. Adherence to the HSE standards may be a partial defence against employment tribunal claims.

of personality characteristics as well as 'individual health factors and social and domestic factors' (Robertson and Cooper, 2011: 73). The direction of causation may be difficult to disentangle here, although the use of panel data such as the British Household Panel Survey (BHPS)[6] can enable researchers to examine the way in which *changes* in health status, for example, impact on wellbeing.

A final point to note is that well-being and job satisfaction are linked to the business cycle (Clark, 2011). Subjective wellbeing is typically higher in booms, boosted by greater satisfaction with job security and pay. This is probably unsurprising to the reader. Less obviously, however, satisfaction with the job itself is higher in recessions – possibly because those remaining in work compare themselves with those who have lost their jobs.

Compensating differentials

Although economists have played a substantial role in recent research using self-reported indicators of wellbeing, for the discipline this is a fairly novel development. Austrian economists (Mises, 1949) preferred to reason from first principles rather than empirics, while the Chicago school advocates such as Milton Friedman (Friedman, 1966) were sceptical of the use of questionnaires and the acceptance of individuals' own accounts of their behaviour and attitudes.

Economic thinking on work begins from a rather different

---

6   The BHPS (which began in 1991) is a large-scale survey which follows the same representative sample of individuals and interviews them on a regular rather than a one-off basis. It can therefore show how a variety of changes in personal circumstances affect people.

perspective. Historically – possibly reflecting the influence of Christian theology, which saw the necessity for work as a punishment for original sin – economists have seen work primarily as a 'disutility', which people try to avoid or minimise. Work is something to be endured and compensated for by payment. This approach, which people on the political right and left have shared to a considerable extent, lies behind debates about the 'work-shy' and the need to incentivise the economically inactive to seek employment.

Mention of compensation should remind economists of the important concept, first developed by Adam Smith in *The Wealth of Nations*, and now known by the term 'compensating differentials'. In Smith's original analysis, he sets out reasons why, even in a highly competitive labour market, pay rates for different jobs are not equalised. This is because jobs differ in many dimensions. Smith writes of the need to compensate for the 'difficulty and expense of learning', which means that people in jobs requiring long, arduous and expensive training and education will typically have to be paid more highly than those in unskilled work if enough people are to be attracted to them. Similarly, he argues that the 'constancy or inconstancy' of employment (i.e. the risk of becoming unemployed) differs from job to job and will be compensated by pay differentials; so too will jobs that carry different degrees of responsibility and trust, or which differ in their 'agreeableness or disagreeableness' (pleasant working conditions, friendly colleagues and personal autonomy on the one hand; long hours, loneliness, exposure to danger, dirt and disease on the other).[7]

---

7 Although if tastes differ between individuals, with some potential employees not finding particular jobs as disagreeable as others, the position is more

The implications of this approach are interesting, and contrast with the 'good job–bad job' dichotomy outlined above. For, if Smith is right, in principle higher pay can compensate for less attractive features of any job. In this view, the same level of job satisfaction and wellbeing could be associated with different combinations of job characteristics, some 'good' and some 'bad'. In a labour market where a wide range of jobs are available, with complete mobility into and out of jobs, there is no reason why indicators of job satisfaction or dissatisfaction should be uniquely associated with particular features of a job, and would be more strongly associated with personal characteristics and circumstances.

There is evidence that compensating differentials do exist. For example, Böckerman and colleagues, using Finnish data, find that higher uncertainty over job security is typically offset by higher wages, other factors being held constant (Böckerman et al., 2010). The principle works the other way round, too: a Canadian study (Helliwell and Huang, 2010) finds that positive characteristics such as the existence of positive and trustworthy management can offset relatively low pay. These authors find that an increase in trust of about one tenth of the scale used in their study is equivalent to more than a 30 per cent increase in income.[8]

This approach can also help to explain why in some studies variables which are assumed to be associated with 'bad' jobs, such as long hours, do not in practice seem to impact negatively on

---

complicated, with the interaction of supply and demand determining whether a premium is paid and, if so, its size.

8   In a similar vein, Birmingham University researchers have recently claimed that those working in family-operated firms have strong positive feelings resulting from mutual loyalty between owners and employees and are prepared to work for lower wages (Siebert et al., 2011).

measured job satisfaction (European Foundation for the Improvement of Living and Working Conditions, 2007a, 2007b). Because people's tastes and personal circumstances differ, they will tend to move into jobs which best suit them. People without family responsibilities, for example, may not be bothered by long hours (Otterbach, 2010), as these are compensated for by higher pay – which was the reason why the job was chosen.

It follows that tight restrictions placed on working hours, as in France, penalise workers who want to work longer and thus paradoxically may result in reduced rather than enhanced job satisfaction for some groups (Wooden et al., 2009). In a similar vein, Leontardi and Sloane (2003) find that some low-paid workers are more satisfied with their jobs than higher-paid workers as they have chosen jobs with other characteristics (job security, work purpose) that they value. The European Commission has claimed, they note, that low-paid jobs are inherently low-quality, 'bad' jobs.[9] But their own findings cast doubt on the idea that there are clearly demarcated 'good' and 'bad' jobs.

A further implication is that restrictions on pay rates, most obviously minimum wage laws, can lead to potentially attractive work opportunities being unavailable. For instance, unpaid or low-paid internships may have the compensating attraction of offering experience and contacts which enable young people to build careers. If minimum wage provisions prevent this, labour market entrants may have to take less satisfying jobs – or end up with none at all.

---

9   Leontardi and Sloane also find that pay is considerably more important to men than to women in determining satisfaction at work. This implies that compensating differentials may be a significant factor in determining the size of the gender pay gap, a point I have made elsewhere (Shackleton, 2008: 46–8).

Is there a 'business case' for employer intervention to improve wellbeing?

What should employers take from this? Bodies such as the Chartered Institute of Personnel and Development and the Work Foundation, together with relevant government departments, often argue that UK management could be doing much more to improve employees' wellbeing at work. But, rather than this being something management should do for moral or ethical reasons, it is frequently argued (Philpott, 2009; Cooper and Dewe, 2009) that they should also do it out of self-interest. Employers are apparently short-sightedly missing the connection between worker wellbeing, performance and productivity. There is said to be a strong 'business case' for the adoption of new strategies and policies to improve the working environment because it will ultimately improve a company's bottom line.

To an economist, the idea that large numbers of companies can be missing out on profitable opportunities to invest in their workforce seems slightly suspicious, reminiscent of many other claims by interested parties[10] of alleged market failure. Very many UK employers, as elsewhere, do have a strong concern for their employees and, indeed, have built competitive advantage as a result of this. But does it follow that other companies are missing out?

Advocates of this view presumably believe that there is some sort of information problem which they aim to remedy. Much

10   Including, in this case, the increasingly influential human resource management profession. The percentage of private sector establishments employing someone with 'human resources' in their job title rose from 22 per cent to 32 per cent between 1998 and 2004. The Chartered Institute of Personnel and Development, the leading professional body, has over 135,000 members today. Twenty years ago it had only 90,000.

use is made of case studies[11] which suggest that introducing new employee-friendly ways of working and engaging employees in managing their own jobs can lead to lower absenteeism, improved customer loyalty, higher productivity and better returns to investors.

Interesting though such instances are, we should be wary of case studies, which are essentially extended anecdotes. There are no proper controls: often the type of employer that is willing to introduce such workplace changes is one that already has a good reputation for the way it treats workers; consequently it attracts a lot of applicants and can pick and choose whom to employ. There-fore it has a positively minded workforce to begin with, one which is favourably disposed to innovation. In employee relations, as in other areas of business, there is a 'first mover' effect: it does not follow that employers attempting to replicate the initiative with less amenable staff will be as successful.[12]

There have been other methodological approaches to building a case for employer interventions to improve wellbeing, including the use of laboratory-based experiments. For example, Oswald and colleagues conducted an experiment which demonstrated

---

11   For instance, Robertson and Cooper in their recent volume (2011) present nine detailed studies of employer interventions to promote wellbeing. Athough each study has a section on 'outcomes and evaluation', however, it is notable that these are all in qualitative terms. There is no quantification of the costs, which in some cases must have been substantial, or the benefits, and thus no demonstration that these initiatives reduced costs or enhanced profitability.

12   It is also worth bearing in mind the possible existence of a 'Hawthorne effect' (named after a famous series of experiments with working practices at the Hawthorne plant near Chicago before the war), whereby *virtually any change* to working conditions can induce an improvement in productivity because the in-dividuals appreciate being singled out for special treatment. Once made routine, however, the new arrangements may have little permanent effect, particularly as new workers come in who were not part of the original innovation process.

that students' performance on a maths test was improved when they were put in a positive mood by viewing a series of clips of comedy performances prior to the task (Oswald et al., 2009). As in this case, however, such experiments do not easily mimic real-life work environments.

Among economists, there has been most interest in using large surveys, such as the UK's periodic Workplace Employment Relations Survey (WERS),[13] to test the idea that supposedly 'best practice' employer policies (which might be expected to improve employees' wellbeing) enhance company performance.

Attention has focused on clusters of indicators of 'high involvement' or 'high commitment' HR practices – such as the provision of off-the-job training, teamworking, job design and enrichment, motivational support, functional flexibility, careful recruitment, performance appraisal and feedback, information disclosure and consultation. The results are a mixed bag, with some positive benefits, but simple conclusions are difficult to reach.

Michie et al. (2008), in a study for the then Department for Business, Enterprise and Regulatory Reform, found that some HR practices have a positive effect on outcomes – for example, the management of absenteeism significantly improves outcomes. A cluster of 'good' practices is associated with product quality. The link with employee attitudes is not universal, however; a positive relationship with their 'HR index' of good practice is found only for the private sector. Moreover, employee attitudes are influenced by a range of non-HR factors (for example,

---

13   WERS is a survey of both employers and employees, enabling researchers to match information about employee attitudes and firm performance. There have been five waves of the survey to date, with another due in 2011.

the improvement in macroeconomic and employment outlook between WERS 1998 and WERS 2004), and 'it appears to be these non-HR factors that are operating through employee attitudes to influence performance' (ibid.: 44).

Brown and colleagues (2008) also find that human resource management practices had little effect on the changes in job satisfaction observed between 1998 and 2004, putting improvements down to increased job security and better industrial relations. They hypothesise that bundles of HR practices include elements that work in opposite directions. Thus 'hard' measures (such as performance appraisal) reduce job satisfaction at the same time as 'soft' measures (more consultation) increase it: the net effect is that these cancel out.

More recently, Wood and de Menezes (2011) note some positives, such as a relationship between consultation (employee 'voice') and job satisfaction, and that certain types of job enrichment improve wellbeing. They also find, however, that motivational support affects neither job satisfaction nor wellbeing, and that formal job guarantees do not significantly affect wellbeing. More generally 'high involvement' management fails to improve wellbeing, possibly as it seems to add to employee anxiety.

Public policy and international comparisons

Some commentators go beyond offering advice to employers and argue for government action to improve wellbeing in the workplace. For example, the Work Foundation (Coats, 2009; Brinkley et al., 2010) makes a case for a mix of 'hard' and 'soft' regulation. 'Hard' initiatives would involve removing the individual opt-out clauses to the Working Time regulations, expanding the Information and Consultation regulations, and requiring companies to provide more extensive information on health and safety performance and job quality. 'Soft' policies would include building on ACAS and HSE standards to promote 'good practice', encouraging union representation at work, and using public procurement criteria to enforce approved standards on government suppliers.

Policy proposals such as these make numerous assumptions – such as the belief that long hours are necessarily a marker of poor job quality, and the view that there is a definable set of 'good practices' – which we have suggested to be open to debate, and probably not a reliable guide to strategy at the level of the individual employer, let alone the economy as a whole.

Expanding the Information and Consultation rules is seen explicitly as a means of 'putting sand in the wheels' (Coats, 2009: 88) of business restructuring; in other words increasing formal employment protection for existing workers. There is a considerable literature (see Skedinger, 2010) to suggest that employment protection for 'insiders' makes it more difficult for new labour market entrants and socially disadvantaged groups to obtain regular work. To the extent that this means higher unemployment for such 'outsiders', it is worth noting the Treasury's observation that 'the negative impact of unemployment on well-being is one of the most striking in the literature. There are also good reasons to think that this is causal rather than correlative' (HM Treasury, 2008: 30).[14]

---

14 Moreover, we should not assume that apparently increased job protection for insiders necessarily has a positive effect on wellbeing. As Skedinger notes, from the evidence it is 'difficult to establish that perceived job security and psychological well-being increase'. In his view this 'may be due to stringent employment protection increasing unemployment duration if one loses one's job ... job-related

Even the softer measures proposed have their dangers: public procurement is already very tightly circumscribed with a host of requirements about environmental sustainability, equality commitments, community employment creation, fair trade, trade union recognition and so forth. Further requirements can only make it more difficult for small firms to compete for government procurement, something which is already a concern to representative organisations.

The Work Foundation, like others seeking to improve employee wellbeing through legislation – for example, in relation to flexible working and parental leave[15] – often makes use of unfavourable comparisons between the UK and other countries. Such comparisons frequently relate only to legal provisions (for instance, laws on dismissal) or simply to factual outcomes (hours worked in different countries, which as we have seen are of ambiguous significance). In the context of this discussion, however, it is important to look at some broader indicators of well-being at work. Table 2 provides several snapshot measures over the last decade, taken from a variety of sources. It is necessary to add caveats to these comparisons: although the same survey questions were used in each cross-country study, national statistical bodies differ in their efficiency and in the representativeness of their sample; questions and concepts used are not necessarily

stress may increase if employment protection brings about management and workplace routines that affect the psychological well-being of workers in a negative way' (Skedinger, 2010: 129–30).

15 Rules concerning entitlements of this kind are often referred to as 'mandates'. They impose costs on employers which are likely to be in excess of the value placed on them by employees. Economic theory suggests that the long-run result is that employees pay for the mandate in lower wages, and this is supported by empirical evidence – for example, Heywood et al. (2005).

compatible from one survey to another; and there may be cultural differences in the way in which respondents reply to identical questions.[16] Nevertheless the results are interesting.

The first column of Table 2 shows that the UK workforce displays low levels of self-reported ill-health: only Ireland does better. This indicator[17] is one of many which could have been included showing a similar picture of a healthy workforce by comparison with most European countries. For example, a European Working Conditions Survey, using a different sampling frame, found that the UK had the lowest proportion (among 31 nations) answering 'yes' to the question 'Does your work affect your health, or not?' We also have one of the lowest work-related accident rates in the European Union. To help maintain this record, evidence shows that health and safety inspections are far more likely to occur in any given period than is the case in any leading European country except Ireland. So the comparative record here appears to be a strong one, and the case for further government intervention seems, on the face of it, very weak.

The second column uses an 'objective' indicator of job security. Although UK workers are by no means easy to dismiss, and are entitled to redundancy payments after a qualifying period, every other European Union country has tighter employment protection legislation than the UK.[18] The corollary of this is

---

16 On this last point, Nicoletti (2006) reports 'bunching' of job satisfaction scores (low standard deviation) in some countries – for example, Denmark and the Netherlands – whereas they are more spread out in others, such as Greece and Italy.

17 This covers males only. The female data present a similar picture and are excluded only for reasons of space. An overall figure would provide misleading comparisons because of the big differences in the proportion of females in the workforce between countries.

18 The OECD's Employment Protection index for 2008 shows the UK at 1.1 on a

Table 2 **Some indicators of wellbeing at work, with comparative rankings***

Country	Percentage of male workers reporting one or more work-related health problem (2007)	Temporary employment as percentage of dependent employment (2008)	Self-reported work stress, average score on five-point scale (2002)	Job satisfaction, average score on seven-point scale (2002)	Subjective wellbeing at work, composite normalised to 10-point scale (2006/07)
Australia	n.a.	n.a.	3.43 [10]	5.04 [15]	n.a.
Austria	16.3 [12]	9.0 [5]	3.55 [12=]	5.51 [2]	5.47 [4]
Belgium	12.8 [11]	8.3 [2]	n.a.	n.a.	5.44 [5]
Denmark	10.8 [8]	8.4 [3]	3.06 [1]	5.42 [3]	5.66 [1]
Finland	20.6 [13]	15.1 [11]	3.41 [9]	5.12 [10=]	5.16 [9]
France	n.a.	14.2 [9]	3.68 [15]	5.07 [12]	5.07 [10]
Germany†	6.6 [4]	14.7 [10]	3.80 [16]	5.27 [6]	4.88 [13]
Greece	7.0 [5]	11.5 [6]	n.a.	n.a.	n.a.
Ireland	3.5 [1]	8.5 [4]	3.22 [5]	5.41 [4]	5.43 [6]
Italy	7.4 [6=]	13.3 [8]	n.a.	n.a.	n.a.
Netherlands	11.2 [9]	18.2 [13]	3.30 [8]	5.12 [10=]	5.60 [2]
New Zealand	n.a.	n.a.	3.49 [11]	5.14 [9]	n.a.
Poland	21.9 [14]	27.0 [15]	3.09 [3]	4.94 [16]	4.43 [14]
Portugal	7.4 [6=]	22.8 [14]	3.10 [4]	5.17 [7=]	5.05 [11]
Spain	5.6 [3]	29.3 [16]	3.23 [6]	5.05 [14]	5.22 [7]
Sweden	11.7 [10]	16.1 [12]	3.58 [14]	5.17 [7=]	5.21 [8]
Switzerland	n.a.	13.2 [7]	3.07 [2]	5.61 [1]	5.50 [3]
United Kingdom‡	5.3 [2]	5.4 [1]	3.55 [12=]	5.06 [13]	4.98 [12]
United States	n.a.	n.a.	3.25 [7]	5.34 [5]	n.a.

Sources: Column 1: Health and Safety Executive using Labour Force Survey data; Column 2: OECD; Column 3: International Social Survey Programme data, reported in Blanchflower and Oswald (2005); Column 4: as Column 3; Column 5: New Economics Foundation using European Social Survey data.
Notes: * For first three indicators lowest value gives highest ranking; for last two highest value is best; † for stress and job satisfaction, West Germany; ‡ for stress and job satisfaction, Great Britain; figures in brackets indicate rankings.

in many cases higher unemployment and in *every* case a higher proportion of people in relatively insecure temporary employment. The case for any further employment protection in the UK needs to be seen against the figures in this column.

The third indicator is a subjective indicator of work stress. The UK comes off relatively poorly in this comparison, although we should be aware of the point outlined in the Box earlier – that work stress is an ambiguous concept as it cannot easily be detached from personal circumstances: two workers in the same environment can react very differently. Any simple link between stress and some of the work environment characteristics mentioned earlier – information and consultation, job protection, union representation – seems difficult to maintain, given that Sweden, France and Germany, where the state regulates these matters much more than in the UK, seem to have higher stress scores. And the USA, with very little government intervention, has a markedly lower stress score.

The next indicator, taken from the same International Social Survey, also has the UK in a fairly low position. There are again, however, some interesting features of this column which make drawing any simple conclusions for policy rather difficult. The USA again does comparatively well on this indicator, despite its low level of regulation. Perhaps more curiously, while for most countries their comparative rankings on the stress and job satisfaction indicator are similar, for Austria, Germany and (most markedly) Poland, their rankings are very different on the two indicators. We might posit that it is possible to have jobs which are stressful but satisfying as in Austria and Germany, but also

---

scale of 0–6. Germany is 2.4, France 2.9, Spain 3.0. Only the USA, at 0.7 on this scale, has a lower score than the UK among developed nations.

to have jobs where there is little pressure but the work is unsatisfying, as in Poland.[19]

The final column shows a more recent measure of overall wellbeing at work. The New Economics Foundation is a strong advocate of using wellbeing accounts to help determine economic policy, and to assist its argument it has used a series of questions in the 2006/07 European Social Survey, which covered 40,000 respondents in 22 countries. In the case of wellbeing at work, it uses six questions[20] to produce a composite index with a ten-point scale. Again the UK is near the bottom, although again Germany is below the UK. Both these countries, incidentally, show lower ratings on this wellbeing at work indicator than they do on the NEF's wider measure of personal wellbeing, which covers such characteristics as having a satisfying life, self-esteem, optimism, resilience, competence and autonomy.

Taking these indicators together, three European countries appear to perform consistently well: Austria, Ireland and Denmark. They are each relatively small economies and have fairly homogeneous populations. They each have comparatively low levels of employment protection, but in other respects their labour market policies differ. Denmark spends much larger amounts on active labour market policies (retraining and reactivating those not in work) than the other two countries, and the

---

19 Conceivably the Polish case is to some extent a hangover from the communist period, when there was little pressure on workers but conditions and pay were poor: as the cynical old line had it: 'We pretend to work, and they pretend to pay us'.

20 The questions covered job satisfaction, work–life balance, interest in the job, proportion of the time the individual experienced stress in their job, the subjective likelihood of becoming unemployed in the next twelve months, and the appropriateness of the respondent's pay.

UK for that matter. Together with Austria, it has much higher labour taxes/social security contributions than Ireland or the UK. Denmark has a very high level of unionisation, around 70 per cent of the workforce, but Ireland and Austria have unionisation rates close to that of the UK, around 30 per cent. So there appear to be few, if any, lessons from these comparisons for the UK. There does not appear to be any obvious set of government policies and accompanying regulation which give other countries a consistent advantage in their citizens' job satisfaction or wellbeing at work.

Conclusions

In a short chapter, it has been possible only to give a brief overview of a large and growing academic literature. Enough has been seen, however, to generate some tentative conclusions about the relevance of this literature to policy debate.

Objective measures such as pay and health indicate that wellbeing at work has increased over time. Subjective measures are more ambiguous, but it is worth reminding ourselves that in most UK studies two-thirds or more of respondents report themselves as being satisfied or very satisfied with their jobs. There is evidence that defined aspects of the work environment have a measurable impact on subjective measures of satisfaction with the job and wider wellbeing at work. There are significant variations in this impact between individuals and groups, however, and this means that we should be sceptical of dividing employment conceptually into 'good' and 'bad' jobs.

The business case does not seem to be convincingly made for employers to adopt a package of human resource practices aimed at improving job satisfaction and wellbeing as a means to higher productivity and improved performance. The 'best practice' cases presented by advocates of change may not be transferable successfully to other employers, and the econometric evidence from large-scale surveys does not support a detailed blueprint for success.

This does not mean that employers should not be on the lookout for ways of making employees happier in their work, but this must be tempered by realism about what is possible and about the consequences for firm performance. In principle it is feasible to increase job satisfaction and worker wellbeing by generous pay hikes, long holidays, expensive training courses and so forth, but there is no guarantee whatsoever that the impact on performance will be sufficient to justify the higher costs. It is salutary to recall that in March 2008 the Royal Bank of Scotland was given an award for being the best UK employer for work and home-life balance. Companies need to develop and protect their business first and foremost: many will hope also to be a good employer, but this cannot be the be-all and end-all.

Finally, does the wellbeing literature support further regulation of the labour market? It seems unlikely. There does not appear to be a set of employment policies adopted by other comparable economies which would lead to unequivocal improvements in job satisfaction and wellbeing, particularly when we consider potential as well as actual employees. Greater employment protection might benefit those in work (although if it significantly harms firms' ability to respond to changes in market conditions, even this isn't the case), but penalises 'outsiders'. And the literature is unequivocal that not having a job at all has strongly negative consequences for wellbeing.

Restrictions on hours, extension of mandatory leave and

similar policies would disgruntle those who would prefer to work more (or lead them to moonlight in the informal economy). It would raise costs, which could discourage private sector job creation at a time when we need to be doing all we can to encourage jobs for those displaced from the public sector. Further monitoring of, or regulations on, health and safety matters would be likely to suffer diminishing returns in the UK context, and would again raise costs.

This chapter has emphasised that the economist's concept of compensating differentials is a useful antidote to interventionist thinking. It suggests that different individuals rate job characteristics differently and that, in seeking a preferred job, individuals will choose a bundle of characteristics, some 'good' and some 'bad', recognising the need for trade-offs.[21] Restrictions on employers' freedom of action through legislation and mandates may prevent them from offering combinations of characteristics which are more highly valued by potential employees than those they are constrained to offer.

Wellbeing at work is important, and something which individuals value more highly as incomes rise, but it is best served by making it possible for employers to offer a range of jobs in all shapes and sizes to suit the varied preferences and aptitudes of a population that refuses to conform to simplistic models of attitudes and behaviour.

---

21 Just as choosing a life partner involves accepting his or her faults or annoying habits in return for the things you love about them, so choosing a job involves the rough with the smooth. In an imperfect world, a search for a job which only has good characteristics is likely to be as fruitless as a search for the ideal partner.

References

Blanchflower, D. G. and A. J. Oswald (2005), 'Happiness and the Human Development Index: the paradox of Australia', *Australian Economic Review*, 38(3): 307–18.

Böckerman, P., P. Ilmakunnas and E. Johansson (2010), 'Job security and employee well-being: evidence from matched survey and register data', Labour Institute for Economic Research (Finland) Discussion Paper 262, http://mpra.ub.uni-muenchen.de/21961/.

Brinkley, I., R. Fauth, M. Mahdon and S. Theodoropoulou (2010), 'Is knowledge work better for us? Knowledge workers, good work and wellbeing', London: The Work Foundation.

Brown, A., A. Charlwood, C. Forde and D. Spencer (2006), 'Changing job quality in Great Britain 1998–2004', Employment Relations Research Series 70, Department of Trade and Industry, December.

Brown, A., C. Forde, D. Spencer and A. Charlwood (2008), 'Changes in human resource management and job satisfaction 1998–2004: evidence from the Workplace Employment Relations Survey', *Human Resource Management Journal*, 18(3): 237–56.

Brown, G. D., J. Gardner, A. J. Oswald and J. Qian (2008), 'Does wage rank affect employees' well-being?', *Industrial Relations*, 47(3): 355–89.

CIPD (2007), *What's happening with well-being at work?*, London: Chartered Institute of Personnel and Development.

Clark, A. E. (2009), 'Work, jobs and well-being across the millennium', IZA Discussion Paper 3940, January.

Clark, A. E. (2011), 'Worker well-being in booms and busts', in P. Gregg and J. Wadsworth, *The Labour Market in Winter*, Oxford: Oxford University Press.

Coats, D. (2009), 'Good work and public policy', in D. Coats (ed.), *Advancing Opportunity: The Future of Good Work*, London: The Smith Institute.

Cooper, C. and P. Dewe (2009), 'Good work – implications for research and policy', in D. Coats (ed.), *Advancing Opportunity: The Future of Good Work*, London: The Smith Institute.

Crafts, N. (2007), 'Living standards', in N. Crafts, I. Gazely and A. Newell, *Work and Pay in 20th Century Britain*, Oxford: Oxford University Press.

European Foundation for the Improvement of Living and Working Conditions (2007a), *Extended and Unusual Working Hours in European Companies*, Luxembourg: Office for Official Publications of the European Communities.

European Foundation for the Improvement of Living and Working Conditions (2007b), *Measuring Job Satisfaction in Surveys – Comparative Analytical Report*, http://www.eurofound.europa.eu/ewco/reports/TN0608TR01/TN0608TR01.pdf.

European Foundation for the Improvement of Living and Working Conditions (2007c), *Work-related Stress*, http://www.eurofound.europa.eu/ewco/reports/TN0502TR01/TN0502TR01.pdf.

Friedman, M. (1966), 'The methodology of positive economics', in *Essays in Positive Economics*, Chicago, IL: University of Chicago Press.

Green, F. (2004), 'Why has work effort become more intense?', *Industrial Relations*, 43(4): 709–41.

Green, F. (2011), 'Job quality in Britain under the Labour government', in P. Gregg and J. Wadsworth, *The Labour Market in Winter*, Oxford: Oxford University Press.

Helliwell, J. F. and H. Huang (2010), 'How's the job? Well-being and social capital in the workplace', *Industrial and Labour Relations Review*, 63(2): 205–27.

Heywood, J. S., W. S. Siebert and X. Wei (2005), 'The implicit costs and benefits of family friendly work practices', IZA Discussion Paper 1581.

HM Treasury (2008), 'Developments in the economics of well-being', Treasury Economic Working Paper 4, November.

Jones, F. and J. Bright (2001), *Stress: Myth, Research and Theory*, Upper Saddle River, NJ: Prentice Hall.

Leaker, D. (2008), 'Sickness absence from work in the UK', *Economic and Labour Market Review*, 2(11): 18–22.

Leontardi, R. and P. J. Sloane (2003), 'Lower pay, higher pay, earnings mobility and job satisfaction', Paper presented at the British Household Panel Survey, July.

Michie, J., N. Zubanov and M. Sheehan (2008), 'Human resource management practices, organisational outcomes and performance: an analysis of WERS 2004 data', Employment Relations Occasional Paper, Department for Business, Enterprise and Regulatory Reform.

Mises, L. von (1949), *Human Action: A Treatise on Economics*, New Haven, CT: Yale University Press.

Nicoletti, C. (2006), 'Differences in job dissatisfaction', Institute for Social and Economic Research Working Paper 2006.42, University of Essex.

OECD (2008), 'Are all jobs good for your health? The impact of work status and working conditions on mental health', in

OECD Employment Outlook, Paris: Organisation for Economic Co-operation and Development.

Oswald, A. J., E. Proto and D. Sgroi (2009), 'Happiness and productivity', IZA Discussion Paper 4645.

Otterbach, S. (2010), 'Mismatches between actual and preferred work time: empirical evidence of hours constraints in 21 countries', *Journal of Consumer Policy*, 33(2): 143–61.

Philpott, J. (2009), 'Good work – good business?', in D. Coats (ed.), *Advancing Opportunity: The Future of Good Work*, London: The Smith Institute.

Robertson, I. and C. Cooper (2011), *Well-being: Productivity and Happiness at Work*, Basingstoke: Palgrave Macmillan.

Shackleton, J. R. (2008), *Should We Mind the Gap? Gender Pay Differentials and Public Policy*, London: Institute of Economic Affairs.

Siebert, W. S., Y. Maimaiti, F. Peng and R. Pearce-Gould (2011), 'HRM practices and performance of family-run workplaces: evidence from the 2004 WERS', Paper presented at the Work Pensions and Labour Economics Study Group Annual Conference, July.

Skedinger, P. (2010), *Employment Protection Legislation: Evolution, Effects, Winners and Losers*, Cheltenham: Edward Elgar.

Waldfogel, J. (2011), 'Family-friendly policies', in P. Gregg and J. Wadsworth, *The Labour Market in Winter*, Oxford: Oxford University Press.

Wood, S and L. de Menezes (2011), 'High involvement management, high-performance work systems and well-being', *International Journal of Human Resource Management*, 22(7): 1586–1610.

Wooden, M., D. Warren and R. Drago (2009), 'Working time mismatch and subjective well-being', *British Journal of Industrial Relations*, 47(1): 147–79.

6 WELLBEING AND THE SIZE OF GOVERNMENT

Christian Bjørnskov[1]

Introduction

The wellbeing and happiness literature of recent years allows social scientists to provide new answers to old questions. One of the most prominent of these questions concerns whether government activities are in some sense 'good'. Instead of defining the value of specific outcomes, based on some theoretical or ideological metric, this literature relies on people's own evaluations of their lives. To the extent that such evaluations are comparable across countries, using answers from satisfaction and wellbeing surveys means that one need not know anything directly about respondents' preferences and values when asking the main question in this chapter: Are people more or less satisfied with their lives in countries in which government 'does more'?[2]

For years, the standard working assumption in economics and political science was that politicians and governments are benevolent and provide public goods and solutions to market imperfections in a best-practice manner. Logically, whatever government spending or regulation one would observe, it would be to the

---

1 I thank Niclas Berggren and an anonymous reviewer for comments that improved the chapter. All remaining errors are of course mine.
2 Note that I use the words happiness, satisfaction and wellbeing as interchangeable concepts throughout.

benefit of the population. In addition, classical welfare economics posited that wellbeing is increasing as consumption increases, but at a decreasing rate. As such, redistribution from citizens with a small marginal benefit from consumption – the relatively rich – to those with a marginal benefit higher than the median – the relatively poor – would contribute positively to overall national wellbeing. This line of thinking, known since the 1940s as the 'Lerner Argument' after the socialist economist Abba Lerner, remains central to the argument made by many current commentators (Lerner, 1944). Their claim is that increased redistribution will cause national *average* wellbeing to increase since the wellbeing loss of the relatively rich caused by redistribution is supposed to be smaller than the wellbeing gain of the poor.

If one were to believe such arguments, increased government spending on public goods and redistributive policies as well as regulation of key markets would necessarily be beneficial to human wellbeing. Yet all such recommendations rest on the set of assumptions that used to be standard *before* the public choice revolution in the social sciences. Those assumptions implied that politicians are benevolent and properly informed about the likely consequences of policies as well as about the preferences of the population. Such assumptions fly in the face of reality.

The large literature on public choice emerging since the 1960s documents, in general, that politicians are self-interested, ideologically biased and influenced by special interests. The main challenge is therefore not to inform politicians about what is the right course of action, but to create an institutional environment in which politicians are unlikely to reach decisions that have adverse economic or social consequences. In the words of James Madison, the challenge is to implement 'a Constitution for Knaves': a set of effective rules that will keep politicians from inflicting harm whether they are benevolent or not (Brennan and Buchanan, 1983). As all constitutions – written or unwritten – fall well short of this goal, one cannot automatically assume as the default that political decisions on government interventions and public expenditures are supposed to have, let alone will have in practice, positive consequences for the wellbeing of the population. A more realistic depiction of politics would tend to lead one to the opposite conclusion.

Instead, a logical, consequentialist requirement for anyone arguing for increasing the size and scope of government activities – more interventions, more activist policy or higher or more progressive taxes must be that they document that the overall size of government is positively associated with national average wellbeing. Whether there are any effects – positive or negative – and whether government policy affects other elements that drive wellbeing differences are the questions explored in this chapter. As argued below, the general answer is no – increased government intervention is not positively associated with increases in wellbeing.

Government ability and incentives

When considering government behaviour, one first has to ask two questions: 1) is government *able* to provide the 'right' amount and extent of public goods and redistribution (if any); and 2) does government have any *incentives* to do so?

An implicit assumption in most active policy proposals coming from happiness scholars seems to be that the government is sufficiently informed about the distribution of preferences in the population. In other words, the government knows what people want. This assumption is inconsistent with the complexity of any modern society, as real-world politicians face a massive Hayekian information problem (Hayek, 1960). In small, local societies, leaders may have sufficient knowledge to direct policies towards those in actual need or towards groups with specific preferences. Yet in only slightly larger societies, it becomes impossible to know enough about the preferences and needs of the population to precisely direct policies in such a way. Instead, politicians arguably need to rely on what the typical or median person in the population prefers.

Yet even if politicians knew the approximate preferences of the median voter, they would still face a heterogeneity problem: although the government might be able to get the right public goods provision to the median voter, a large share of people would find specific public goods over-provided and another share would find them under-provided. Consequently, most people would be paying the wrong amount of taxes for public goods provision targeted merely to the median voter. They would be paying for not only the wrong level of public goods but also the wrong mix.

A second problem is that of how decisions are reached in politics. Dictatorships may arguably be able to focus policies on meeting the desires of relatively narrow elites while providing enough order and public goods to prevent social unrest. In principle, democracies ought to be different and provide a wider set of necessary public goods in accordance with the needs and preferences of the population. Owing to information problems, being able to do so may nevertheless be prohibitively difficult. In addition, politicians often have incentives that aggravate this problem and undermine their willingness to try.

Tullock (1981) famously provided an explanation for why democracies tend to reach stable decisions, which rests on log-rolling. This explanation also gives an intuitive reason for why democracies may reach too many decisions at too high a cost to voters, and thus why government spending above a 'night-watchman' level in many cases can be detrimental to national wellbeing. Tullock realised that to reach decisions that are supported by a majority and are unlikely to be overturned by the next government, one has to combine support for different policy proposals such that all groups will vote for the combined package. This implies that relatively narrow groups, all with their own preferred spending item, can push their policy agendas through Parliament even though, individually, those policies may be to the detriment of the majority of the population. The need to reach a majority thus implies that overall spending is likely to be larger than preferred by most of the population and that the structure of spending will not reflect its preferences. Instead, spending will reflect the preferences of those groups that have political influence and which are likely to be pivotal in political bargains.

Further problems also point in the direction of excessive spending that effectively would lower the wellbeing of most of the population. Politicians deciding on government spending arguably exploit voters' income as a fiscal commons, as excessive spending today can be covered by excessive taxes tomorrow (Mueller, 2003). Such spending does not contribute to wellbeing and may even reduce it as voters relinquish control of their personal income. Now-classic studies also document that spending may be too high owing to politicians' log-rolling, their preferences for 'visible' government projects, and the lobbying activities of special interests (Tullock, 1959, 1981; Olson, 1965).

Likewise, as government grows, so does the power of a bureaucratic elite with incentives to maximise budgets, personal staff or both (Niskanen, 1971). As bureaucracies grow, controlling them consumes more resources, such that a growing government automatically triggers disproportionally higher expenses (Mueller, 2003).

One could argue that democracy allows voters to control politicians better, which would counteract the tendencies towards excessive government. The public choice literature also documents, however, that the behaviour of politicians aiming to be re-elected contributes to excessive spending and resource misallocation, which is facilitated by a large share of voters that are 'rationally ignorant' (Downs, 1957). Politicians trying to win elections have strong incentives to be seen to be 'doing something' for specific groups in society. As such, subsidising important groups of voters or special interests causes excessive spending as well as additional spending that is allocated to purposes other than providing beneficial public goods. In total, much public choice theory and Austrian information economics implicitly predict that government spending and other activities will either be irrelevant or directly detrimental to wellbeing, when above some absolutely necessary level.

Main determinants of national happiness

When confronting theory with the real world, the first question to ask concerns the factors that determine the differences in levels of wellbeing across nations. A growing literature has explored a large number of different factors but found relatively few to be robustly associated with wellbeing; Bjørnskov et al. (2008a), Frey (2008) and Dolan et al. (2008) provide recent surveys. A number of these factors are, in principle, at least partially within the control of the government and thus subject to political influence.

Most studies find, not surprisingly, that unemployment is associated with lower levels of wellbeing. A number of other economic features are positively associated with wellbeing: trade openness; measures of the investment climate; and the quality and limited extent of regulations all affect how people evaluate their own lives. As outlined in the next section, however, the direction in which governments typically affect these factors is not consistent with the wellbeing of the population.

Another main influence is the overall quality of formal institutions, defined as the degree of fairness and efficacy of legal systems, the police and public bureaucracies together with how inclusive and democratic political systems are. Legal institutions that protect the life and property of citizens tend to matter for all countries, while those that are rich enough to have overcome problems of deep poverty also experience wellbeing gains from introducing democracy (cf. Helliwell and Huang, 2008; Bjørnskov et al., 2010). In addition, a set of what are often termed 'informal institutions' affects wellbeing. Among such factors are generalised trust in other people, religious beliefs and network activities (Bjørnskov et al., 2008a; Helliwell, 2006).[3]

Although early studies indicated that these factors are subject to government policy, more recent studies suggest that the most robust determinants of happiness – trust and religiosity – are not

3   While recent research clearly finds that these factors contribute to wellbeing, one cannot reject the conclusion that wellbeing also affects trust and voluntary network activity. This potential feedback occurs, however, without any government intervention. The communist experience suggests that direct government involvement may undermine the links between trust, networks and wellbeing.

affected by government policy. Likewise, the most effective legal institutions tend to be politically independent, a point made abundantly clear by British development after the 1689 Glorious Revolution. The exception to the rule seems to be dramatic totalitarian changes, as is clearly visible for the formerly communist countries. Virtually all studies identify having a communist past as one of the most robust and strongly negative influences on national wellbeing (Hayo, 2007; Dolan et al., 2008). Decades with a command economy not only reduced trust levels and left countries poorer and with deficient legal and regulatory institutions, but also had direct effects on the population. Comparing countries with similar current objective living standards, but with and without a communist past, reveals a wellbeing deficit in formerly communist countries of between one half and one point on a ten-point scale (Bjørnskov et al., 2008a, 2010). Evidently, the communist experience demonstrates the limit to government involvement before it seriously detracts from wellbeing.

Yet two issues were disputed from the beginning of this literature. The first was whether higher average incomes are associated with more subjective wellbeing. The second was whether increasing government involvement in the economy makes a positive difference. An important qualification when discussing these issues is that the main influence of objective material improvements on subjective wellbeing is usually limited to two to three years, after which people have updated their aspirations sufficiently to eliminate the effects of most positive surprise changes (Frey and Stutzer, 2004; Stutzer, 2004; Bjørnskov et al., 2008a).

In principle, strongly expansionary fiscal policy could *temporarily* increase happiness levels but have the opposite effect in the long run as citizens discover the fiscal illusion. After that, however, the long-run limit to the positive impact of government interventions applies. Where that limit is has been a major question since the early days of happiness studies. One of the first studies to pose this question directly was Veenhoven (2000), which found no association between the size and scope of the welfare state and average wellbeing. Veenhoven also rejected the idea that welfare states somehow reduce the inequality of wellbeing. Other studies are even more negative.

Bjørnskov et al. (2007) test the influence of three types of government spending on happiness: capital investments, total spending and final consumption (all spending except transfers). In a comparison across 74 countries, they find that government final consumption negatively affects happiness levels and that the negative influence occurs regardless of how effective government bureaucracy is or how democratic the country is. The authors paradoxically also find, however, that left-wing and centre voters are more negatively affected by government spending. The results in Bjørnskov et al. (ibid.) indicate that increasing government spending by about a third, which corresponds to the difference between spending in France and more prudent Germany, would cause a direct reduction in happiness of about three percentage points, or roughly 5–6 per cent.

The same authors, in a different research design, replicate this result in a comparison of 90,000 individuals from around the world (Bjørnskov et al., 2008a). In addition to supporting previous findings, they document that when focusing on the poorest third of national populations, government final consumption is a statistically significant and strongly negative contributor to happiness, while the happiness of the richest third of a population is not so clearly associated with the size of government. In their comparisons of individuals around the world, Bjørnskov et al. find that increasing government spending by 10 per cent reduces the subjective wellbeing of citizens in the poorest third of the population by about 1–1.5 per cent. Their results also show, however, that while right-wing voters are affected to twice the extent of left-wing voters, having a right-wing government to some extent alleviates the negative effect. Evidently, excessive government intervention mainly harms the happiness of poorer parts of society while leaving richer segments no better off.

A related issue is how far from voters decisions are made, i.e. how centralised government is. Frey (2008) argues that decentralised decision-making is directly associated with happiness, as it produces 'procedural utility' (i.e. people value influence per se). Another way in which decentralisation could affect happiness, and in particular through the effects on happiness of government decisions, derives from Hayek's information economics.

Hayek (1960) argued that in order for government interventions to benefit people, governments would need access to a large amount of specific information. Not only would they need to know the way the economy works, but also the true preferences of the population and the distribution of those preferences. If one-size-fits-all policies are implemented to fit the preferences of the median voter, for example, they might be unsuitable to the large share of the population with preferences for more or less of whatever the policy is supposed to deliver. In addition, such policies need to be financed and thus imply opportunity costs. These problems will tend to be smaller the closer to voters political decisions are made (Mueller, 2003). With decentralised decision-making, gathering precise information on voter preferences and policy costs is more possible and specific problems can be addressed that are not within the effective reach of national policies. One would therefore expect that the costs (benefits) of government spending and interventions are larger with more (less) centralised decision authority.

One of the few papers to distinguish between centralised and decentralised decision-making, Bjørnskov et al. (2008b: 150), concludes that 'Local autonomy, however, increases well-being only insofar as it neutralizes the detrimental impact of the government sector.' In other words, decentralised governments are likely to make decisions and implement policies that are, on average, *neutral* with respect to the wellbeing of their citizens. Centralising political decision-making, on the other hand, makes it more likely that the size and scope of the public sector grows to the extent of being significantly detrimental to wellbeing (cf. Frey, 2008).

The other main question is whether economic development increases national wellbeing. This topic is covered by Sacks, Stevenson and Wolfers (in this volume), who show that economic growth leads to higher subjective wellbeing in the long run. One of the main drivers of growth, economic globalisation, also causes higher levels of subjective wellbeing over and above its effects on growth (cf. Bjørnskov et al., 2008a; Tsai, 2009).

At the individual level, people tend to get used to being richer – at least to some extent – when national wealth has reached a relatively moderate level. Likewise, most people adjust their expectations somewhat downwards when they are consistently disappointed (Stutzer, 2004; Dolan et al., 2008). As such, reductions in private consumption resulting from higher taxes to finance government spending may in principle cause only a temporary reduction in wellbeing until individual expectations and aspirations have adjusted. In practice, however, Di Tella et al. (2003) show that people are not likely to adjust their expectations fully. Because of this, economic growth is likely to lead to higher wellbeing overall.

The government sector and its active role in society could thus cause losses of happiness in the long run because of its effect on economic growth. Activist government policies and a growing public sector are likely to undermine both growth and globalisation (e.g. Fölster and Henrekson, 2001; Bergh and Henrekson, 2011), and thus slow down the already slow trend towards greater wellbeing. Given this, the apparently popular case for active government involvement in increasing wellbeing seems misdirected. As noted above, a number of studies find no basis for the claim that government spending is positively associated with happiness. High government spending instead tends to reduce growth and may also be harmful to other factors contributing to happiness.

In addition, the potentially positive effects of material improvements may be less likely to be visible in the wellbeing of countries. As a sizeable share of the population provides answers that are close to the maximum happiness level in survey questions, the inability to place one's assessment of wellbeing higher than the top category of the questionnaire constrains the surveys at the top end, thereby making it more difficult to measure the real effects of improvements within the group of countries that already has high levels of wellbeing (see Ormerod and Johns, 2007; Stevenson and Wolfers, 2008). The real effects of government spending in rich democracies may thus be underestimated.

Government redistribution

Another defining characteristic of so-called modern welfare states is the high degree of redistribution, either through direct in-kind provision of private goods or through monetary transfers and progressive taxation. Both types would imply a larger government size, the former through more direct government production and the latter through higher levels of taxation. Yet government arguably provides private goods in a much less efficient way than the free market.

Regardless of whether government provides public goods, redistributes income or directly provides private goods, the size of the public bureaucracy is likely to increase, representing a classic 'leaky bucket' problem: that whenever government intervenes, an indirect consequence is a loss of overall economic efficiency (Okun, 1975). A direct test of government's ability to spend effectively on redistribution is therefore to explore the potential association between the outcome of that spending or taxation – income inequality – and happiness. One has to be careful in making such assessments, however: if government implements some form of policy of redistribution, its potential wellbeing consequences will have to more than supersede its negative effects on overall efficiency. Most studies do not take this into account, but test the direct effect of redistribution or spending on wellbeing, disregarding its efficiency effects. The literature therefore merely asks whether there is a positive and direct association between redistributive policies and wellbeing.

Despite the much-publicised claims made by, e.g., Layard (2005), there appears to be no such association. For example, the large-scale empirical exercise in Bjørnskov et al. (2008a) finds no evidence of any correlation between income inequality and happiness; see also Snowdon (in this volume). The same is the case in Napier and Jost (2008), who take another approach to analysing the wellbeing effects of income inequality in the USA. Their results suggest that inequality affects only people placing themselves at the far ends of a political left–right scale. The effects are such, however, that the gains from redistribution to very left-wing respondents are entirely offset by the wellbeing losses suffered by very right-wing respondents. Schwarze and Härpfer (2007) conclude that redistribution across the German *Länder* is at best inconsequential, and may reduce the wellbeing of the middle class. While redistribution to relatively poor Germans does not have positive effects and the costs of redistribution appear to be negligible to the relatively rich, most actual financial costs of redistribution are likely to be borne by the middle class.

More fundamentally, testing the basis for the popular redistribution–wellbeing association – the Lerner argument – Cullis et al. (2011) find that there are no appreciable decreasing returns to income in wellbeing. In other words, while the basis for the idea that redistribution leads to increased average wellbeing is that income matters more to the relatively poor, this seems not to be the case. As such, the only likely effects of redistribution would be the losses from the leaky bucket: that is the bureaucratic costs of redistributing income.

Conclusions

What appears to be the unequivocal conclusion to be drawn from the sober, scientific part of the wellbeing literature is that larger government does not imply a happier population. Indeed, when a growing battalion of social scientists sympathetic to government interventions engage in wellbeing research and fail to find empirical evidence in favour of such interventions, it seems safe to conclude that more or larger government is not associated with better wellbeing. As Ruud Veenhoven honestly concluded against his own political preferences more than a decade ago, the characteristics of welfare states neither create wellbeing, nor do they make the distribution of such wellbeing more equal (Veenhoven, 2000). A further decade of research has confirmed this conclusion despite popular claims that government interventions can and do create happiness.

On the contrary, the large and growing literature finds either no consequences of government policies or direct negative effects of large government (cf. Bjørnskov et al., 2008a, 2008b). Yet even if there are no direct effects, there is reason to worry that increasing the size of the government sector and its active role in society could cause losses of happiness in the long run. As documented by Sacks, Stevenson and Wolfers in this volume, economic growth leads to happiness in the long run. Likewise, economic globalisation also tends to contribute to subjective wellbeing (see Tsai, 2009). Activist government policies and a growing public sector are likely to undermine both growth and globalisation (e.g. Fölster and Henrekson, 2001; Bergh and Henrekson, 2011), and thus slow down what is already a slow trend towards more wellbeing that may be difficult to track in rich countries.

As such, the apparently popular case for an active government that creates happiness rests on very shaky foundations. Although the UK and other countries have begun directing their statistical agencies towards informing governments on what to do, the evidence suggests that additional spending in the government sector is *at best* likely to be pure waste, as evaluated by citizens' happiness. Instead, when asking what government can do for you in terms of happiness, the proper answer seems to be an echo of Adam Smith's famous 1755 lecture: 'peace, easy taxes, and a tolerable administration of justice; all the rest being brought about by the natural course of things' (cf. Frey and Stutzer, 2000; Bjørnskov et al., 2010). In the present political circumstances, however, there are few votes to be had from such promises. Policies actually conducive to average happiness are neither sexy, nor likely to attract more votes.

References

Bergh, A. and M. Henrekson (2011), 'Government size and growth: a survey and interpretation of the evidence', *Journal of Economic Surveys*, forthcoming.

Bjørnskov, C., A. Dreher and J. A. V. Fischer (2007), 'The bigger the better? Evidence of the effect of government size on life satisfaction around the world', *Public Choice*, 130: 267–92.

Bjørnskov, C., A. Dreher and J. A. V. Fischer (2008a), 'Cross-country determinants of life satisfaction: exploring different determinants across groups in society', *Social Choice and Welfare*, 30: 119–73.

Bjørnskov, C., A. Dreher and J. A. V. Fischer (2008b), 'On decentralization and life satisfaction', *Economics Letters*, 99: 147–51.

Bjørnskov, C., A. Dreher and J. A. V. Fischer (2010), 'Formal institutions and subjective wellbeing: revisiting the cross-country evidence', *European Journal of Political Economy*, 26: 419–30.

Brennan, G. and J. M. Buchanan (1983), 'Predictive power and the choice among regimes', *Economic Journal*, 93: 89–105.

Cullis, J., J. Hudson and P. Jones (2011), 'A different rationale for redistribution: pursuit of happiness in the European Union', *Journal of Happiness Studies*, 12: 323–41.

Di Tella, R., R. J. MacCulloch and A. J. Oswald (2003), 'The macroeconomics of happiness', *Review of Economics and Statistics*, 85: 809–27.

Dolan, P., T. Peasgood and M. White (2008), 'Do we really know what makes us happy? A review of the economic literature on the factors associated with subjective well-being', *Journal of Economic Psychology*, 29: 94–122.

Downs, A. (1957), *An Economic Theory of Democracy*, New York: Harper.

Fölster, S. and M. Henrekson (2001), 'Growth effects of government expenditure and taxation in rich countries', *European Economic Review*, 45: 1501–20.

Frey, B. S. (2008), *Happiness: A Revolution in Economics*, Cambridge, MA: MIT Press.

Frey, B. S. and A. Stutzer (2000), 'Maximizing happiness?', *German Economic Review*, 1: 145–67.

Frey, B. and A. Stutzer (2004), 'Reported subjective well-being: a challenge for economic theory and economic policy', *Schmollers Jahrbuch*, 124(2): 191–231.

Hayek, F. A. (1960), *The Constitution of Liberty*, Chicago, IL: University of Chicago Press.

Hayo, B. (2007), 'Happiness in transition: an empirical study of eastern Europe', *Economic Systems*, 31: 204–21.

Helliwell, J. F. (2006), 'Well-being, social capital, and public sector; what's new?', *Economic Journal*, 116: C34–C45.

Helliwell, J. F. and H. Huang (2008), 'How's your government? International evidence linking good government and well-being', *British Journal of Political Science*, 38: 595–619.

Layard, R. (2005), *Happiness: Lessons from a new science*, London: Penguin.

Lerner, A. P. (1944), *The Economics of Control: Principles of Welfare Economics*, New York: Macmillan.

Mueller, D. C. (2003), *Public Choice III*, Cambridge: Cambridge University Press.

Napier, J. L. and J. T. Jost (2008), 'Why are some conservatives happier than liberals?', *Psychological Science*, 19: 565–72.

Niskanen, W. A. (1971), *Bureaucracy and Representative Government*, Chicago, IL: Aldine Atherton.

Okun, A. M. (1975), *Equality and Efficiency: The Big Tradeoff*, Washington, DC: Brookings Institution.

Olson, M. (1965), *The Logic of Collective Action*, Boston, MA: Harvard University Press.

Ormerod, P. and H. Johns (2007), 'Against happiness', *Prospect Magazine*, 133, April.

Schwarze, J. and M. Härpfer (2007), 'Are people inequality averse, and do they prefer redistribution by the state? Evidence from German longitudinal data on life satisfaction', *Journal of Socio-Economics*, 36: 233–49.

Stevenson, B. and J. Wolfers (2008), 'Economic growth and subjective well-being: reassessing the Easterlin Paradox', *Brookings Papers on Economic Activity*, 1: 1–87.

Stutzer, A. (2004), 'The role of income aspirations in individual happiness', *Journal of Economic Behavior and Organization*, 54: 89–109.

Tsai, M.-C. (2009), 'Market openness, transition economies, and subjective well-being', *Journal of Happiness Studies*, 10: 523–39.

Tullock, G. (1959), 'Problems of majority voting', *Journal of Political Economy*, 67: 571–9.

Tullock, G. (1981), 'Why so much stability?', *Public Choice*, 37: 189–205.

Veenhoven, R. (2000), 'Well-being in the welfare state: level not higher, distribution not more equitable', *Journal of Comparative Policy Analysis*, 2: 91–125.

PART THREE: MADE HAPPY BY GOVERNMENT OR FREE TO PURSUE HAPPINESS?

7 THE UNBEARABLE LIGHTNESS OF HAPPINESS POLICY

Marc De Vos[1]

The political rediscovery of happiness

Happiness has been one of man's desires throughout the ages, and philosophers have grappled with the idea of happiness since the dawn of civilisation. From the eighteenth century onwards, happiness has been broadly equated with pleasure and well-being, a subjectivist and hedonistic understanding that departs from the more austere and transcendent ideals of earlier times (McMahon, 2006). The Enlightenment also elevated the promotion of happiness to the level of public policy. A famous passage in the American Declaration of Independence classifies 'the pursuit of happiness' as an unalienable human right. The revolutionary French Constitution of 1793 declared general happiness to be the goal of society. Utilitarian thinkers of the late eighteenth and early nineteenth centuries defined 'the greatest happiness for the greatest number' as the overall yardstick for public policy choice (Bentham, 1789).

It should come as a surprise, then, that happiness did not figure prominently in mankind's most recent and most predominant societal experiment to promote wellbeing: the welfare state. The traditional welfare state is primarily an engine for insurance

---

1   The opinions expressed in this article are personal and cannot be attributed to the Itinera Institute, its staff or trustees.

against life's tribulations. Its underlying drive is material redistribution in search of fairness and justice. Its programme is essentially protective in nature and paternalistic in purpose, aiming to provide material security for entire populations. Personal wellbeing was part of the equation, but only as an expected natural by-product of the essential welfare goals of munificent income security and/or material support. Much of the welfare state was and remains fundamentally materialistic, not hedonistic.

This is changing. The pursuit of happiness is back in vogue. Across academe – in economics, in political science, in psychology, and in epidemiology – the exploration of happiness or generic 'subjective wellbeing' is positively booming. Happiness economics is a genuine hype in the post-crisis economic profession. Reams of new research, a string of recent books and a hyperactive conference circuit have turned happiness into arguably the hottest topic of contemporary social science.

There is much to be said for this rediscovery of happiness. It can add a quality dimension to our prominent quantitative measures of human development, such as economic growth, income evolution, employment figures, poverty rates or education scores. In the field of economics, it is part of a useful evolution to broaden the understanding of human action and nuance the stereotype of human beings as self-interested, rational, utility-maximising agents. Personal happiness is unquestionably important in life and therefore relevant as a topic of public concern. Improving our understanding of happiness will improve our understanding of societies. Adding happiness to the array of perspectives on policy issues can insert a human angle and force us to ponder effects that would otherwise remain ignored.

But can and should the actual promotion of happiness be a

purpose or subject of policymaking as such? Should the pursuit of happiness become politics? Some of the towering figures of the happiness revival advocate nothing less than a radical happiness agenda. We are told that 'We need a revolution in government. Happiness should become the goal of policy, and the progress of national happiness should be measured and analysed' (Layard, 2005a). Economics should equally be revolutionised and become *happynomics*: 'it is – or should be – about personal happiness' (Frey et al., 2008). The first comprehensive monograph on happiness politics is now available for use (Bok, 2010). Politicians are paying attention and have entered the happiness game. The 27 nations that form the European Union officially plan to move 'beyond GDP', seeking to complement economic output with environmental and social indicators, including quality of life and wellbeing (European Commission, 2009). This pan-European agenda comes in the slipstream of a global United Nations initiative to benchmark overall human development.[2] The Organisation for Economic Co-operation and Development (OECD) – the major official policy body of the developed world – for its part has launched a 'Better Life Initiative', with the purpose of comparing wellbeing across its 34 member-countries.[3]

At the national level, the pursuit of happiness is increasingly entering the political mainstream. At the request of the French president, a high-profile crop of economists has proposed to measure economic progress by more than the usual growth figure, adding parameters for sustainability, happiness, the quality of life and the environment (Stiglitz et al., 2009). In the UK, Prime Minister Cameron and his Conservative Party want to devise

2   www.hdr.undp.org.
3   www.oecdbetterlifeindex.org.

an index of national wellbeing, in an effort to care about 'joy in people's hearts' instead of 'money in people's pockets' (Office for National Statistics, 2011). In Germany, both the federal parliament and Chancellor Merkel are following France's lead to reassess GDP and embrace national happiness *über alles*.

In a recent essay, I have challenged the burgeoning happiness agenda from several perspectives (De Vos, 2011). For this collection, I will focus on two critical assumptions of the current happiness revival: that 'happiness' or 'subjective wellbeing' can be sufficiently defined and measured as to make it a reliable policy instrument and that its promotion is morally desirable.

Measuring happiness measurement

The problems of measuring happiness

Switching from the private pursuit of happiness to the public promotion of happiness requires a determination of what happiness actually is, and the ability to organise its promotion collectively. It is there that the happiness dream meets reality in the shape of three major obstacles that undermine both its practicality and its legitimacy: one methodological, one ethical and one political. I will address these in succession.

From a methodological perspective, no defensible happiness policy can really be considered without a clear understanding of its subject. Happiness apostles are eager to stress the scientific nature of their endeavours. Happiness is labelled as a 'new science' rooted in empirical observation.[4] It is claimed we now know, at

---

4   Layard has entitled his seminal book *Happiness: Lessons from a new science*.

long last, what really makes people happy. But any unbiased observer who encounters happiness studies for the first time cannot help being struck by how crude and unsophisticated they actually are. Almost all the available empirical happiness research to date is based on surveys that ask individuals how happy or how satisfied they are with their lives. These surveys typically involve general questions probing happiness or life satisfaction, such as:

- Taken altogether, how would you say that things are these days?
- Do you think of yourself as very happy, pretty happy or not too happy?
- Have you been feeling reasonably happy all things considered?
  Sometimes specific issues are probed, such as:
- Have you lost much sleep over worry?
- Have you been able to concentrate on things?
- Have you felt you are playing a useful part in things?
- Have you felt capable of making decisions about things?
- Have you felt constantly under strain?
- Have you felt you could not overcome your difficulties?
- Have you been able to enjoy your normal day-to-day activities?
- Have you been able to face up to your problems?
- Have you been feeling unhappy and depressed?
- Have you been losing confidence in yourself?
- Have you been thinking of yourself as a worthless person?
  The World Values Survey, for example, asks:
- Taking all things together, would you say you are: very happy; quite happy; not very happy; not at all happy?; and

- All things considered, how satisfied are you with your life as a whole these days?

Other variants, such as the Gallup World Poll, employ a ladder analogy. Interviewees are asked to imagine a ladder with each rung representing a successively better life. Respondents then report the 'step' on the ladder that best represents their life. Such lines of questioning remind one more of the shrink's sofa than of meticulous data mining. But they are nonetheless invoked to 'scientifically' diagnose the state of the human condition (Oswald, 2010).

Should we use individual subjective measures of happiness to determine public policy for everyone?

The immediate conclusion is that our so-called 'scientific' happiness data are nothing more than a collection of tentative happiness gauges, summarily offered by fallible respondents, in response to very crude questions, and interpreted by fallible researchers, some of whom turn out to have a personal political agenda. Should we take all this as rock-solid evidence to supplant overall economic progress with somebody's grand happiness plan? There are several reasons to be very hesitant at least, well beyond the intrinsically vague and imprecise nature of the happiness surveys as such.[5] It is widely recognised that responses to happiness surveys are *inherently subjective and relative*. Feelings of personal wellbeing are influenced by infinite personal and cultural biases. Each and every individual faces life's predicaments

---

5   For a pedagogical and descriptive overview, see Bok (2010: ch. 2).

differently. Our biological and neurological make-up differs: happiness and unhappiness, at the end of the day, are about brainwaves. Education and cultural norms vary. Societal attitudes and expectations differ. All of these affect the way different people judge similar situations on their personal happiness scale. None of these transpires from the current happiness meters. One records *subjective* wellbeing and therefore by definition accepts that responses will be subjective. But should we really use subjective individual data as scientific intelligence to determine public policy for everyone?

Measured happiness is context specific

Not only are our crude happiness measurements subjective and relative, they are also *inherently unreliable* to some extent. People may be motivated to manipulate reports of their own wellbeing, either downplaying or exaggerating wellbeing according to the context and the purpose of the enquiry. If 'Gross National Happiness' were to be used to measure wellbeing, citizens could strategically adapt their life satisfaction responses in order to influence policies to their liking. It is also recognised that respondents to happiness surveys tend to be unduly susceptible to fluctuations of moment-to-moment mood. Subjective reports of wellbeing moreover suffer from our tendency to conform our responses to implicit standards of assessment or comparison we acquire through culture and society (Loewenstein and Ubel, 2008). These standards also evolve in time, making the entire exercise of comparing happiness over time inherently problematic. Furthermore, the standard of judgement people use when reporting their level of happiness is contextual and malleable. For instance, when people are asked to report how well they are doing *relative to their own and their parents' past,* self-reported levels of happiness rise dramatically (Hagerty, 2003). The whole mechanism of grading happiness in relation to wealth – *the* key statistic fuelling the entire 'beyond-GDP' logic – suffers from the cardinal methodological flaw that no respondent can keep on increasing his/her personal happiness level beyond 'very happy', whereas income continues to rise over time. The purported disconnect between increased wealth and increased happiness is thus effectively organised by the very statistical mechanism that is supposed to report it. Is this scientific?

We cannot know in sufficient detail what causes happiness

Next up is the perennial Achilles heel of all statistical enquiries: the distinction between correlation and causation. It is not enough to fathom the connection or disconnection between wealth and happiness. For any judgement to be scientifically admissible, one also needs to establish the causes of the observed relationship. Almost the entire collection of happiness surveys fails on this account alone. Not only are these surveys crude and partly unreliable recordings of subjective emotions, they are also unable to link the recorded sentiments to a comprehensive set of possible sources of happiness or distress. There are some recognised categories of correlation, linking happiness to money, work, health, family relationships, community and friends. But beyond these broad generalisations, many possible factors that influence subjective wellbeing still await exploration. There is some evidence that the link between wealth and happiness is direct and causal: i.e. not dependent on other factors besides increasing wealth (Pischke, 2011). But this undermines, rather than supports, the thesis that we should move beyond wealth to create more happiness. In any event, the limits of our statistical comprehension alone should put any comprehensive happiness agenda on the back burner for now. We simply do not know enough of what drives (un)happiness in a given society.

If people are the best judge of their own wellbeing, why question personal economic behaviour?

Happiness surveys are obviously not entirely random. They cannot be discarded as irrelevant. Some studies have tried to verify recordings of subjective happiness, through repetitions or by connecting them to more objective factors. They have found relevant degrees of reliability (Krueger and Schkade, 2007; Oswald and Wu, 2010). But these efforts to rationalise the irrational remain sketchy and superficial. Happiness research essentially relies on rudimentary surveys because it has nothing better. People are reckoned to be the best available judges of their own happiness (Frey et al., 2008: ch. 1). This may well be true, but that does not make it a legitimate basis for a wholesale policy agenda. Quite the contrary: if people's words on ephemeral feelings are to be taken for granted, then why question the much more reliable and verifiable source of their actions? Why question people's consumer decisions and desire for prosperity, but accept their version of happiness? If happiness scholars are right that people are the best judge of their own lives, shouldn't we rely on the preferences revealed by their judgement to buy the next iPhone (Wolfe, 2008)?

Happiness measures are a 'snapshot'

And it doesn't stop there. Happiness surveys are a collection of snapshot impressions, asking respondents to commit their immediate feelings to paper. We all know, however, that true meaning and value in life transpire only over time and in retrospect. This fundamental fact of human wisdom is totally left out of the equation. Available happiness estimates are about instant and real-time sensations, not about sustained contentment. This is a crucial caveat to make, from two perspectives. On the one hand, it steers subsequent happiness policy towards short-term satisfaction, begging the question whether this is truly the kind of happiness our society should seek to foster. We will engage this issue below. On the other hand, it makes the proponents of happiness policies over growth policies ignore the very same obstacle that brings them to question economic growth in the first place: our human nature is able to adapt to circumstances over time. While they question wealth for its supposed lack of impact on happiness in the long run, they survey happiness as an instantaneous and real-time phenomenon.

More wealth – so the happiness movement claims – fails to produce ever more wellbeing because its beneficiaries gradually grow accustomed to it. But the very same adaptation process plagues their alternative of promoting happiness. While happiness surveys record one-off snapshots at different intervals, other research convincingly demonstrates that circumstances and events often have a surprisingly small impact when happiness is instead measured over time. By and large, happiness levels appear remarkably impervious to changes in the external environment. People both report and experience approximately the same level of happiness regardless of their social or personal wellbeing. For example, numerous studies have found that people with severe chronic health conditions report happiness levels that are close to those reported by healthy persons, and which are much better than healthy people believe their moods would be if they had those conditions. Such gradual adaptation of our feelings of wellbeing to different circumstances is neither universal nor complete, but it is strong and persistent.[6] Circumstances that we can change through actions or policy thus clearly have a much smaller lasting influence on our subjective happiness than given factors such as genetic disposition. That raises an uncomfortable existential question for the happiness movement: if we shouldn't care about economic growth because people adapt to wealth, why should we bother about happiness when people adapt to fortune and misfortune alike? Perhaps happiness preachers do not like market-driven growth and prefer the political orchestration of happiness instead. Should we accept their preference as morally superior?

A shallow form of happiness

There are roughly two types of happiness. So-called *eudaimonic* wellbeing (from the Greek *daimon* – true nature) harks back to Aristotle and his conviction that true happiness is found by leading a virtuous life and doing what is worth doing, with the realisation of our human potential as the ultimate goal. Then there is the happiness that Aristotle found vulgar: the *hedonic* wellbeing derived from mere personal pleasure and contentment, traditionally associated with Jeremy Bentham and his strictly utilitarian approach to life. What kind of happiness is sought in the

---

6   See the overview in Gilbert (2006) and also Loewenstein and Ubel (2008).

current revival? One of its key proponents puts it this way: 'By happiness I mean feeling good – enjoying life and wanting the feeling to be maintained. By unhappiness I mean feeling bad and wishing things to be different' (Layard, 2005a: 12). The doyen of US happiness scholars describes a happy person as one that 'experiences life satisfaction and frequent joy, and only infrequently experiences unpleasant emotions such as sadness or anger' (Ed Diener, quoted in Bok, 2010: 9). This approach is profoundly hedonistic. The happiness surveys, with their focus on personal sentiment and instant sensations, are equally biased towards the hedonistic side. They are the 21st century's equivalent of the 'hedonometers' envisaged as the scientific measure of human contentment by Bentham's nineteenth-century utilitarian heirs.[7] Other approaches to happiness exist, but the overwhelming inclination of contemporary happiness research is towards the hedonic-subjective idea of happiness.

If hedonic pleasures are to constitute the bedrock of public policy, we risk committing our societies to a course of instant and often superficial gratification, instead of real fulfilment and progress. If hedonic contentment is to be its goal, then the burgeoning happiness revolution may well prove to be very conservative indeed: it will end up promoting the very materialism and consumerism their proponents so often associate with the GDP addiction they seek to undo. Relaxing, shopping, watching TV, socialising and having sex: these are activities that typically generate a high level of hedonic happiness. Household work, professional work and commuting are associated with low average levels of happiness (Layard, 2005a: 15). Are we then to

---

7   'Economics discovers its feelings', *The Economist*, 19 December 2006.

promote an empty lifestyle of transient pleasures? Whatever the orientation, one thing is abundantly clear: no happiness policy can be considered without a priori normative and moral choice on the type of happiness we want to promote. Are we to promote hedonistic contentment, notwithstanding its short-term and fleeting nature, or do we instead seek true happiness over the longer term, even if that requires short-term sacrifices and even unhappiness? Should we really seek to promote pleasant feelings and to minimise painful feelings, or instead distinguish bad pleasures from good ones, and bad pain from good pain? This requires a profound reflection which the happiness literature has largely ignored so far.[8] The baffling claim that happiness is self-evidently good and therefore by definition the right guide for public policy and private decisions alike (ibid., 113, 115) simply does not stack up. John Stuart Mill's famous aphorism on nineteenth-century utilitarianism equally applies to its present-day reincarnation: 'Better to be Socrates dissatisfied than a fool satisfied'. In the meantime, however, decades of hedonic happiness data are being piled up and, before long, risk shaping the terms of the happiness debate as a self-fulfilling prophecy without prior reflection.

The inescapable ethical dimension of the happiness debate goes well beyond the scope of individual human development. What matters for individuals has an impact on society at large. Irrespective of whether we favour hedonic or austere happiness as the standard for personal wellbeing, we should also take into consideration its potential aggregate effect for society and mankind in general. Should we douse society with a standard dose of comfortable pleasure? Or should we recognise that many

---

8   For an overture, see Nussbaum (2008).

a human triumph was born from bleak adversity? Do we not risk undermining the energy of human progress by seeking to provide happiness for all? Few among us would favour deliberately organising hardship for the sake of promoting greatness. But we cannot ignore the fact that the active public promotion of hedonic happiness is bound to undermine some of the melancholy and dissatisfaction of the human condition that has so often spurred creativity and progress in many fields. We cannot fail to recognise that individuals who reach the highest level of happiness typically do not possess that nagging sense of unfulfilled ambition that pushes others to heights of innovation and worldly success (Bok, 2010: 51). We should not forget that the success story of capitalistic innovation is rooted in a culture of hard work, personal sacrifice and delayed gratification (McCloskey, 2006). An agenda obsessed with hedonic pleasure is a strategy for decline.

The spartan or puritan among us will therefore certainly deplore the erosion of progress – whether material, scientific or artistic – that is bound to arise when we cover humanity with a warm blanket of happiness (Wilson, 2008). The most balanced among us should at least recognise the dilemma and ponder carefully the potential societal side effects of personal happiness promotion, no matter how well intentioned. It is a dilemma many of us will recognise as parents in raising children. Do we indulge them in the latest fashion, TV show and video game, or do we instead install discipline, stimulate hard work, teach the limits of money and the value of earned success? Do we embrace the Chinese 'Tiger Mother' famously portrayed in a current bestseller, pushing our children to the limits of their ability in iron discipline, hoping they will appreciate and value it later in life (Chua, 2001)? Or do we accept failure and take off the pressure, even when it undermines their future potential? Similarly in education: do we emphasise discipline, learning and the transfer of knowledge, or are schools really there to make children happy and assertive (Loveless, 2006)? Hedonic contentment may be the easy ride and the more pleasurable one while it lasts, but it may also end up eroding overall progress and leave the individual frustrated in later life. To put it plainly and simply: happiness cannot be the sole measure if human beings are to survive over time (Epstein, 2008/09).

Beyond societal progress, there is the issue of *societal cohesion*. Turning individual happiness into a policy goal implies an individualistic policy orientation. It may remove us from a narrow-minded obsession with individual interest, but only to replace it by a focus on individual pleasure. In both cases the prism remains the individual and the policy individualistic in purpose, if not in method. In this, our current happiness extollers again echo the world-view of their nineteenth-century utilitarian predecessors. Jeremy Bentham famously stated that 'the community is a fictitious body' and that the interest of the community is 'the sum of the interests of the several members who compose it' (Bentham, 1789). This atomistic approach to society is the philosophical prerequisite for the utilitarian agenda of hedonic happiness promotion: you cannot posit individual happiness as the ultimate aim without accepting the individual as the ultimate yardstick. This, however, boils down to societal nihilism. Any society, in the end, rests upon a moral order – whether articulated or unspoken – that balances freedom and coercion, and settles the relation between personal impulses and community requirements (Bell, 1996: ch. 6). By focusing on personal happiness alone, we ignore societal cohesion and its moral foundation at our peril. Fun is not and cannot be pursued in a vacuum. Our societal contract contrasts self-interest with public interest. Consequently, we inevitably will have to limit the promotion of happiness to what is accepted as proper and desirable. Here again, the happiness programme necessitates a normative and moral enquiry which its enthusiasts fail to acknowledge.

Happiness, freedom or justice?

This brings me to *societal fairness*. Postulating happiness as a public policy goal, rather than as the liberty of each individual, is a normative political decision with massive moral implications. Is our key societal objective to produce happiness, or justice? Are the policy implications of a happiness agenda compatible with our understanding of justice and fairness, or not? Those who associate justice with the welfare state's redistributionist programme may well prefer *Justland* over *Happyland* (Vandenbroucke, 2011). Most happiness preachers speak happiness but mean welfare and redistribution, apparently convinced that the two are one and the same.[9] They may be surprised to learn that subjective wellbeing depends much more on living standards than on state welfare (Veenhoven, 2000), that rising income inequality has coincided with declining happiness inequality (Stevenson and Wolfers, 2008a), or that the effect of inequality on the poor's happiness depends much more on a society's cultural attitude towards inequality than on inequality per se.[10] The happiness way will not

---

9   See the list and the quotes in Wilkinson (2007: 2–4).
10   The effect of inequality on the poor is statistically insignificant in the USA but larger in Europe, owing to different societal attitudes towards inequality: see Alesina et al. (2004).

necessarily be the path of egalitarianism and income redistribution so typically favoured by the missionaries of the welfare state. Indeed, the basic assumption that wealth does not bring everlasting happiness instead suggests that happiness policies will be less materialistic in emphasis. Choices will undoubtedly have to be made. The more conservative or libertarian minded will be quick to point out that more happiness is also closely related to more economic and political freedom, and that the opportunity for merited success beats any welfare programme on the happiness scale (Wilkinson, 2007: ch. 3).

The moral case for a deliberate happiness agenda is therefore clearly far from straightforward. Any happiness policy – no matter how shaky or solid its statistics, no matter how sound or foolish its economics – will face a difficult moral trade-off currently ignored by the swelling chorus of happiness adepts. Much of the current happiness tale is told in an amoral virtual reality shaped by the factual registration of personal sentiments. It needs a healthy dose of ethical and philosophical reflection to set its moral bearings if we are to translate empirical findings into policy arguments. There will always be two sides to the morality coin, and no happiness policy can therefore be conceived as a straightforward ethical enterprise.

More fundamentally, however, no matter how clever or balanced our construction of happiness may be, we cannot escape the fact that it will fail to capture a wide range of values and dimensions that people legitimately care about. If life is about much more than money, as most of us will readily admit, it is clearly also about much more than mere personal happiness. Any happiness policy by definition succumbs to an egotistic self-indulgent bias that ignores other fundamentals of the human condition, not only on the personal level but also in the context of marriage, family and society at large. From an ethical point of view, society should clearly be concerned not only with having its citizens living the good life, but also a life that is good. This moral dimension has so far been lost in today's hedonistic happiness revival. In any case, every programme to promote happiness by definition will have to determine what it considers sufficiently valuable for promotion, while ignoring all other factors, no matter how valuable they may be for its intended beneficiaries. At the end of the day, happiness policy therefore becomes the political determination of happiness.

Poor but happy?

Any attempt to disconnect growth from happiness also has uncomfortable ethical implications of its own. A government that prioritises happiness over growth is a government that is ready to accept a lower standard of living for its citizens. And our ability to adapt to economic conditions works both ways: we can adjust to misery as well as to wealth. During the recent economic crisis, for instance, Americans' assessments of their personal wellbeing nosedived after the 2008 Wall Street meltdown but recovered to stable (and slowly rising) levels by mid-2009, despite rising joblessness and diminishing wealth. As Princeton's Angus Deaton showed in a study published in autumn 2011, the arrival of Valentine's Day had more of an effect on the wellbeing of Americans as measured by the happiness surveys than did a doubling of unemployment (Deaton, 2011). Are we then ready to seek personal happiness and remain oblivious to economic malaise? Will we ignore the plight of the unemployed because their happiness levels adjust to their hardships?

When a society fails to offer economic opportunity and jobs, people derive more wellbeing from non-economic factors. But are those who question the value of economic growth ready to impose the happiness framework of poor countries upon rich ones? Making happiness the overriding aim of public policy would bring us to accept, and even to justify, hardship and decline. This could hardly be called responsible public policy or a moral improvement.

This is the implicit (and often explicit) aim of the happiness scholars: to drive us to value non-material goods over wealth. But this goal is based on a simplistic and paternalistic understanding of how human beings think about our own contentment. After all, if ever-increasing wealth yields only uncertain rewards of happiness, why do so many of us try so hard to achieve it?

The truth is that increasing wealth may bring a degree of satisfaction that is difficult, if not impossible, to measure by polling personal happiness. Many of us undoubtedly strive for wealth because it enables us to achieve other goals – for ourselves, our families, and our communities – that the happiness surveys simply do not register. A focus on happiness over growth would thus curtail our ability to use material prosperity for non-material goals, thereby limiting our freedom to achieve contentment. By relying on a simplistic understanding of happiness, the happiness advocates would narrow and flatten our actual pursuit of it. There is a clear moral case against the bland promotion of happiness over growth.

Conclusion

For every human being, indeed for most living creatures,

wellbeing and happiness matter tremendously. The pursuit of happiness is a natural and crucial part of the human existence, as philosophers have recognised for many centuries. A state of personal happiness clearly can benefit society as well. Happy people on average have more productive and successful careers (Oswald et al., 2009), are more willing to engage in the risk-taking of the successful entrepreneur (Bosman and van Winden, 2006), live longer and healthier lives (Diener and Chan, 2001), and even drive more safely (Goudie et al., 2011). There is thus a strong case for integrating a happiness perspective into policy reflection. Valuing happiness also brings us closer to the essentials of life, and may thus help to supersede some of the materialistic biases of existing policies.

Unfortunately, however, happiness is not only promoted as an additional factor for consideration in the process of political decision-making. A hard core of very visible happiness enthusiasts is advocating a return to a utilitarian past, defending the greatest happiness of mankind as the ultimate common good and its promotion as the overarching goal of public policy. In this chapter, I have argued that this happiness agenda comes with weak credentials and unclear motives. Elsewhere, I have also exposed dangerous assumptions on the role of economic growth as an instrument for wellbeing, and doubtful goals that offer little more than an entitlement bonanza or worse (De Vos, 2011).

It is time to acknowledge these flaws and put the political promotion of happiness into the right perspective. We should not switch from a perceived obedience to GDP to a real obedience to coarse emotional indicators. We need to recognise the inherent fallibility of happiness meters and consider their limits as reliable instruments. We need to understand how current happiness surveys are biased towards fleeting emotions of hedonic pleasure that, if they are to form the lightning rod for policy, will set humanity on a track of amoral gratification and overall decline. We need to square the reign of happiness with that of justice. We should be concerned not only with living the good life, but also a life that is good. We need to acknowledge that happiness meters fail to register how many of us seek wealth to achieve other goals – for ourselves, our families or our communities. We need to realise that happiness meters ignore the underlying factors that determine subjective wellbeing, among them the powerful forces of economic freedom and self-determination.

Making the promotion of happiness the pinnacle of policy priorities is as easy in principle as it is hard in practice. It is easy to accept as a broad policy platitude. It is hard to reliably and verifiably go from platitude to action. The problem of the happiness agenda lies not so much in its aim as in the inherent fallibility and arbitrariness of its implementation. There is only so much one can know about subjective wellbeing and only so much one can do about it through policy. At the point of action, the politics of happiness will be more about the preferences of its authors than of its subjects.

References

Alesina, A., R. Di Tella and R. MacCulloch (2004), 'Inequality and happiness: are Europeans and Americans different?', *Journal of Public Economics*, 88: 2009–42.

Bell, D. (1996), *The Cultural Contradictions of Capitalism*, 20th anniversary edn, New York: Basic Books.

Bentham, J. (1789), *Introduction to the Principles of Morals and Legislation*.

Bok, D. (2010), *The Politics of Happiness*, Princeton, NJ: Princeton University Press.

Bosman, R. and F. van Winden (2006), *Global Risk, Investment and Emotions*, DP 5451, Center for Economic Policy Research.

Brooks, A. (2010), *The Battle. How the Fight between Free Enterprise and Big Government Will Shape America's Future*, New York: Basic Books.

Chua, A. (2011), *Battle Hymn of the Tiger Mother*, London: Penguin Press.

Deaton, A. (2011), 'The financial crisis and the wellbeing of Americans', NBER Working Paper no. 17128.

De Vos, M. (2011), 'Reclaiming happiness from politics', Itinera Institute Discussion Paper.

Diener, E. and M. Y. Chan (2011), 'Happy people live longer: subjective well-being contributes to health and longevity', *Applied Psychology: Health and Well-being*, 3: 1–43.

Epstein, R. (2008/09), 'Happiness and revealed preferences in evolutionary perspective', *Vt. L. Rev.*, 33(559): 559–83.

European Commission (2009), *GDP and Beyond. Measuring progress in a changing world*, COM (2009) 433 final.

Frey, B. et al. (2008), *Happiness. A Revolution in Economics*, Cambridge, MA: MIT Press.

Gilbert, D. (2006), *Stumbling on Happiness*, New York: Alfred Knopf.

Goudie, R. et al. (2011), *Happiness as a Driver of Risk-Avoiding Behavior*, CESifo WP Series no. 3451.

Hagerty, M. R. (2003), 'Was Life Better in the "Good Old Days"? Intertemporal Judgments of Life Satisfaction', *Journal of Happiness Studies*, 4(2): 115–139.

Krueger, A. and D. Schkade (2007), *The Reliability of Subjective Well-being Measures*, CEPS Working Paper no. 138.

Layard, R. (2005a), *Happiness: Lessons from a new science*, London: Penguin.

Layard, R. (2005b), 'Happiness is back', *Prospect*, 108: 14–21.

Loewenstein, G. and P. A. Ubel (2008), 'Hedonic adaptation and the role of decision and experience utility in public policy', *Journal of Public Economics*, 92: 1795–810.

Loveless, T. (2006), 'How well are American students learning?', *Brown Center Report on American Education*, II(1), October.

McCloskey, D. (2006), *The Bourgeois Virtues*, Chicago, IL: University of Chicago Press.

McMahon, D. (2006), *Happiness: A History*, New York: Atlantic Monthly Press.

Nussbaum, M. (2008), 'Who is the happy warrior? Philosophy poses questions to psychology', *Journal of Legal Studies*, 37: 81–112.

Office for National Statistics (2011), *Measuring National Well-being*, London: ONS.

Oswald, A. (2010), *Emotional Prosperity and the Stiglitz Commission*, IZA Discussion Paper no. 5390.

Oswald, A. and S. Wu (2010), *Objective Confirmation of Subjective Measures of Well-being: Evidence from the USA*, IZA Discussion Paper no. 4695.

Oswald, A., E. Proto and D. Sgroi (2009), *Happiness and Productivity*, IZA Discussion Paper no. 4645.

Pischke, J.-S. (2011), *Money and Happiness: Evidence from the Industry Wage Structure*, NBER WP 17056.

Stevenson, B. and J. Wolfers (2008a), *Happiness Inequality in the United States*, IZA Discussion Paper no. 3624.

Stevenson, B. and J. Wolfers (2008b), *Economic Growth and Subjective Well-being: Reassessing the Easterlin Paradox*, IZA Discussion Paper no. 3654.

Stiglitz, E., A. Sen, J.-P. Fitoussi et al. (2009), *Report by the Commission on the Measurement of Economic Performance and Social Progress*, Paris: CMEPSP.

Vandenbroucke, F. (2011), *Geluk als doelstelling, doelstelling als geluk. Een pleidooi voor vitaliteit*, Redenaarsconcert 'De Triomf van de Menselijkheid'.

Veenhoven, R. (2000), 'Well-being in the welfare state: level not higher, distribution not more equitable', *Journal of Comparative Policy Analysis*, 2: 91–125.

Weber, M. (1904/05), *The Protestant Ethic and the Spirit of Capitalism*, first published in German.

Wilkinson, W. (2007), *In Pursuit of Happiness Research. Is It Reliable? What Does It Imply for Policy?*, Cato Policy Analysis no. 590, Washington, DC: Cato Institute.

Wilson, E. (2008), *Against Happiness: In Praise of Melancholy*, New York: Farrar, Straus and Giroux.

Wolfe, A. (2008), 'Hedonic man. The new economics and the pursuit of happiness', *New Republic*, July.

8 LESSONS FROM AUSTRIAN AND PUBLIC CHOICE ECONOMICS FOR THE HAPPINESS DEBATE

Peter J. Boettke and Christopher J. Coyne

Introduction

Over the past few decades economists have paid increasing attention to how 'happiness' or 'subjective wellbeing' affects economic outcomes. The origins of what has become known as 'happiness economics' can be traced to Richard Easterlin's (1974) well-known study which gave rise to the 'Easterlin paradox'. In its simplest form, this paradox states that above a certain level of income, economic growth does not improve human welfare. Starting in the 1990s, the Easterlin paradox received renewed attention resulting in a burgeoning literature on the topic (see Frey and Stutzer, 2002a, 2002b).

Economists working on happiness economics typically define subjective wellbeing or happiness by general satisfaction with life. In order to capture wellbeing, economists often rely on surveys, which ask some variant of the question: 'How happy are you with your life?' Other survey questions aim to understand whether people value relative or absolute income by asking something along the lines of: 'Would you rather earn £50,000 in a world where others earn £25,000 or would you rather earn £100,000 in a world where others earn £200,000?' Researchers then compare the responses to these questions, both across societies and against economic outcomes, in the hope of determining what factors influence the overall level of happiness and satisfaction. Many studies have found support for Easterlin's 'progress paradox' (see Frey and Stutzer, 2002a, for a review). If incomes have gone up over time, researchers wonder, why has happiness stayed relatively flat?

Researchers have provided two main explanations for this paradox. One explanation is that people judge their level of wealth not in absolute terms, but rather in relative terms. This implies that increases in welfare are not just a matter of everyone's income increasing. Instead, an increase in one individual's income must be relatively higher than everyone else's in order for it to have a real effect on the welfare of the individual in question. This means that even if the general level of income increases, it will have little effect on any one person's happiness in the absence of relative changes.

Another explanation is the 'hedonic treadmill' effect, which refers to the tendency of people to return to some baseline level of happiness. As a result, increases in wealth yield smaller increases in satisfaction and happiness than one would expect. It is not necessarily the case that people are unhappy, but rather that happiness is fleeting. This is because as people become wealthier their expectations also increase, meaning their overall level of happiness remains flat. This implies that even as people work harder to achieve happiness, they ultimately remain in the same place. Related to the hedonic treadmill explanation, researchers argue that the continual striving to increase wealth, which leads only to temporary increases in satisfaction, results in negative consequences in other aspects of life. For example, more effort expended to earn more income results not only in a short-term spike in happiness, but also less time to spend with family, friends and members of the community.

A strong set of policy conclusions has emerged from these explanations for the progress paradox. For example, numerous happiness researchers call for some form of taxation on labour and luxury goods (see Frank, 1999; Layard, 2005). The logic behind this tax is as follows. If relative wealth is what matters, then an increase in one person's wealth, relative to others, must harm other people. This is the equivalent of a negative externality, which is typically solved through a tax that forces people to internalise the cost of their actions. In theory, a tax would raise the cost of consuming labour or luxury goods, overcoming the causes of the progress paradox discussed above. That is not all. Proponents of this type of taxation add that there is another benefit because the money raised through taxes can be used for such 'public goods' as better schooling, recycling, more art programmes, healthcare and public transportation, among others (see Frank, 1999: 249–61; Griffith, 2004: 1392; Layard, 2005: 47). At first blush, these policy prescriptions seem like a win-win, for proponents promise not only more happiness, but more public goods as well.

We, however, are sceptical. The purpose of this chapter is to raise some conceptual and practical issues with the study of happiness economics and the associated policy recommendations as outlined above. Our analysis draws on concepts from Austrian economics and public choice economics.

Among other things, Austrian economics emphasises the subjectivity of costs and benefits; the importance of dispersed and context-specific knowledge of time and place, which is crucial to economic coordination and cannot be known or collected by planners; and that the market is a continuous process characterised by productive entrepreneurial activities. Public choice economics extends the core assumptions of the economic way of thinking to politics. In doing so it assumes that those in politics have self-interested agendas and that they respond to incentives just like private actors. The main implication is that we cannot assume that those in politics are benevolent and other-regarding. Instead we must consider the constraints and incentives they face in designing and implementing policies, even if those policies are motivated by the best of intentions.

We proceed as follows. The next section considers some conceptual issues with happiness economics. We then turn to some of the practical issues with happiness economics, examining efforts to design and implement policies based on this research. The final section concludes with an alternative way of thinking about happiness and public policy.

Conceptual issues

What is happiness?

This question has perplexed philosophers for centuries. Wilkinson (2007: 12) identifies four possibilities for what 'happiness' may entail: life satisfaction; experiential or hedonic quality; some yet to be determined state that falls outside of life satisfaction or experiential states; and wellbeing. The happiness literature typically focuses on one of these possibilities or attempts to merge all four together. Surprisingly, scholars working in the area of happiness economics rarely if ever engage in an in-depth discussion of exactly what it is they are trying to capture versus what it is they are actually capturing through their research tools.

This is an important question because people may be willing

to make trade-offs between specific margins of happiness. As Wilkinson writes, 'Not only do people give different weights to the various elements of happiness and well-being, people don't even agree about what they *are*' (ibid.: 15, emphasis in original). The absence of a universal definition of happiness creates problems for measuring actual happiness since supposed measures of happiness may be capturing different and competing aspects. Furthermore, the lack of a clear definition of happiness poses problems for those designing policies that supposedly maximise wellbeing. How can potential alternative 'happiness policies' be evaluated in the absence of a common and agreed-upon benchmark of happiness? Policies that attempt to maximise notions of happiness on one margin may end up costing people on other margins that truly matter to them. In total, policies that increase happiness on one margin could decrease overall happiness.

Can happiness be compared between individuals and across time?

The notion of happiness is not static across individuals at a specific point in time. As Wilkinson writes, 'In addition to systematic differences between individuals, the way people report their happiness is highly sensitive to context, threatening the reliability of surveys' (ibid.: 8). This implies that comparing survey responses across people at a point in time is problematic. Yet many happiness studies compare responses across countries to gauge the relative happiness of societies. Putting aside issues of aggregation, which are by no means unimportant, it is unclear that happiness can be measured across people any more than 'utilities' can be compared across economic actors. Because individual values are subjective, we cannot meaningfully compare them across individuals or even across time for the same individual in any objective way. As James Buchanan notes, 'utility is a subjective phenomenon, and it is not something that can be externally or objectively measured' (Buchanan, 1969: 9). Even though we may be able to compare the relative incomes of two individuals, we cannot say anything meaningful about their relative satisfaction or the wellbeing that those individuals derive from that income. Lionel Robbins made a similar point when he wrote, *'There is no means of testing the magnitude of A's satisfaction as compared with B's* ... Introspection does not enable A to discover what is going on in B's mind, nor B to discover what is going on in A's' (Robbins, 1932: 124, emphasis in original).

While comparing happiness between people at a point in time poses one set of problems, comparing happiness across time poses a separate set of issues. While much of the happiness economics literature focuses on framing issues – as evidenced by the emphasis on the aforementioned 'hedonic treadmill' effect whereby those that are relatively wealthy expect more – to explain differences in wellbeing, it neglects the fact that such framing issues will cause individual respondents to have varying understandings of what the notion of happiness entails. As the circumstances change, so too does their very understanding of the notion of happiness and wellbeing. Kling (2004) illustrates this point when he notes that 'People a few hundred years ago had no idea what it was like to live with indoor plumbing, abundant food, and antibiotics'. Of course, actual happiness survey data is not available over hundreds of years, but Kling's point with this example is that as circumstances change, so too do notions of happiness. How can we compare the happiness of respondents in 1970 to those in 2011? Technological advances have changed life on so many margins that it is unclear how we can be sure that surveys are capturing the same concept of happiness across time. And if they are not capturing the same notion of happiness, how can we meaningfully compare survey responses across time periods and conclude that happiness has changed or remained constant?

Is there a fixed stock of status?

A core concept in happiness economics is the role of 'status', which refers to one's position relative to others. Just as relative income matters for wellbeing, happiness scholars contend, so too does relative status. Scholars point out that social status is a 'positional good' – a good whose value is a function of its desirability in the eyes of others. Positional goods are zero-sum from the standpoint that if one person possesses status, others cannot also hold that same position. This matters for the study of happiness because when one person obtains a certain status, it imposes negative costs on others because they cannot obtain that same status. Those with a relatively lower status are worse off compared with those in higher-status positions.

This logic underpins many of the policy prescriptions emerging from the happiness literature. For example, Frank (1999) argues that individuals, in seeking relative status, place too much focus on tangible goods (i.e. house size, cars, vacations, etc.) while neglecting intangible goods (i.e. commuting time, family time, etc.). It is the (over)emphasis on accumulating tangible goods, while underemphasising the importance of intangible goods, which leads to the underlying paradox. The main implication is that public policy should be oriented such that it raises the relative cost of obtaining tangible goods. With the relatively higher cost of tangible goods, individuals will tend to increase their consumption of intangible goods.

This line of reasoning, however, assumes that status is fixed. It is true that if there is a fixed amount of status, then competition for status goods is zero-sum. But why should we assume that the amount of status is given and fixed? If we allow for time and entrepreneurship in our analysis of status, one could easily argue that the array of status goods is constantly emerging and evolving. Under this line of reasoning, old forms of status are discarded, existing forms of status evolve, and new forms of status emerge. Cowen (2000) argues that markets continually create new margins of fame as new technologies and opportunities emerge. If status is viewed as a continually evolving process instead of as some fixed 'stock', then it is unclear that status is as big a problem as happiness scholars would lead us to believe.

Practical issues

What goods count and how much?

Happiness scholars often talk of taxing the 'pollution' created by status and relative income. Layard notes that when one person earns more income others suffer because they earn less in relative terms. The person that gains, however, 'does not care [that] he is polluting other people in this way ...' (Layard, 2005: 247). A tax, it is argued, can force the higher earner to internalise the costs of their pollution. This logic sounds reasonable to many. After all, who likes pollution? A deeper consideration of the implications of taxing relative increases in income, however, should make one at least somewhat sceptical of these policy implications.

To understand why, consider what taxing the 'pollution' created by increases in relative income would actually mean. Taken literally, it would mean that all productive entrepreneurial activity would need to be taxed since it leads to an increased income for the entrepreneur. The economics of profit and loss indicate that profits result when an alert entrepreneur combines resources in a manner that customers value. This is why customers are willing to turn over their money for the good or service. A tax, however, is a means of discouraging an activity. A tax on productive entrepreneurship would lead to fewer productive activities which would make people worse off by reducing innovation and positive-sum interactions. Even if productive entrepreneurial activities do generate costs in terms of 'pollution' by increasing relative incomes, this cost must be weighed against the benefits in terms of increased wealth and all that comes with it – higher standards of living, better education, lower levels of disease, less infant mortality, etc. (Lee, 2005). Given that future entrepreneurial activities cannot be known or measured, it is unclear how one would carry out such an analysis in any meaningful way.

Proponents of a 'happiness tax' on productive activities may claim that this is unreasonable. They may claim that they do not want to tax all activities, but instead just certain luxury items and high-status activities. But how are these luxury and status items to be determined and weighted in practice? Should only for-profit activities be taxed? What about non-profit opportunities such as the Gates Foundation, which lead to status in the world of philanthropy? What about medical research aimed at curing disease? After all, discovering a cure for a disease is surely a positional good which generates pollution according to Layard's logic. The question of what goods and activities count as pollution generators must be addressed by policymakers who design and implement policies based on happiness research. This means that public choice economics – the application of the economic approach to politics – comes to the forefront.

An array of public choice models indicate that politics suffers from self-interested officials and bureaucrats, as well as interest groups which attempt to influence and capture policy for their own benefit at the expense of the broader population (see Mitchell and Simmons, 2004). Policies, even if driven by the best of intentions, cannot be designed in a vacuum. Instead, policies are designed in a setting where a variety of self-interested political agents are competing to design policies that satisfy their own personal agendas. We need to ask ourselves what incentives policymakers face when designing and implementing happiness policies. What are the feedback mechanisms if mistakes are made? What are the relevant interest groups attempting to influence and capture policy? These are the types of questions which public choice economics forces us to consider when considering the realities of happiness policies. Unfortunately, issues of public choice are rarely, if ever, discussed in the happiness literature. This is surprising given the strong policy conclusions that many happiness scholars proffer.

Finally, we must point out an irony in the policies offered by happiness scholars. The political elites that control the design and implementation of happiness policies are holders of high-status positions. Likewise, happiness scholars who offer advice to governments on how to design and implement policies to maximise happiness similarly hold positions of the highest status.

The status is derived from having the influence and power to tell citizens what they can and cannot consume, and in what amounts, in the name of maximising happiness. Surely political elites and happiness scholars, given their concern for the happiness of others, would support a large tax on their own incomes and consumption to reduce the significant pollution they generate.

Negative unintended consequences

A major issue faced by policymakers is the knowledge problem. As F. A. Hayek (1945) emphasised, the economic problem facing society is not one of simply allocating given resources. Instead, the key issue is how to best secure and utilise the unique knowledge of 'time and place' that is dispersed throughout society. At any point in time an individual can possess only a small piece of the knowledge that is present in society. Hayek concluded that a market economy, with an unhampered price system, was the best means of coordinating economic activities. Given Hayek's insight, one realises that government interventions are based only on the limited knowledge of policymakers. As a result, it is unclear that specific policies can be designed that will have the desired effect because interventions will generate negative unintended consequences which policymakers, given their necessarily limited knowledge, could not have possibly anticipated.

We noted above how a tax on a specific behaviour will reduce the amount of the taxed behaviour. Kirzner (1979) highlights the 'stifled discovery process' whereby a government intervention distorts or obscures alertness to existing or possible profit opportunities. By raising the cost of productive entrepreneurial activities to reduce 'pollution', happiness taxes also distort alertness to profit opportunities that could generate benefits. These negative consequences are unobservable and unmeasurable because of their counterfactual nature. In other words, we do not know what would have transpired without the tax. Kirzner (ibid.) also notes how government intervention can result in a 'wholly superfluous discovery process', which occurs when an intervention results in entrepreneurial actions that are not anticipated, potentially resulting in negative outcomes. For example, as policymakers design and implement happiness policies there is no doubt that various interest groups will expend resources to attempt to influence policy. These behaviours are profitable to the interest groups, but destructive at a social level because they represent wasted resources allocated to transfers instead of productive activities.

Moreover, it must be realised that government policies aimed at maximising happiness are non-neutral. As highlighted by Hayek (1976), questions of distribution are often misplaced in political economy because they assume a fixed pie that is being divided up according to rules of distribution that are judged as fair or not. Hayek's objection was not that fair divisions are not desirable. His criticism was that the rules of fair division are non-neutral with regard to the incentives and information associated with production. In other words, the size of the pie being divided is a function of the way we divide the pie. Interventions aimed at redistribution shift the incentives and information faced by those engaged in the process that produces the goods being redistributed. Policies based on the size of the pie at one point in time will influence the size of the pie in future periods.

What 'public goods'?

As noted earlier, many happiness scholars conclude that a policy of taxing labour and certain goods is a way to resolve the progress paradox. Not only will this resolve the paradox, they contend, but the tax revenue can then be used to fund public goods that benefit society. Little focus or discussion, however, ever surrounds how policymakers will actually make decisions regarding the allocation of tax revenue to these public goods. To understand the practical issues at work, consider the standard logic behind public good provision.

A pure public good has two specific characteristics. The first characteristic is that it is non-rivalrous, meaning that one individual's consumption does not reduce others' ability to consume the good. The second characteristic is that it is non-excludable, which means that once the good is produced, individuals cannot be prevented from consuming the good. In theory, public goods are under-supplied on the unhampered market because of issues associated with free-riding and pricing. The standard solution to problems associated with public goods is some combination of government provision and government subsidies to correct for the shortfall. Practical difficulties emerge, however, in the movement from theory to practice to solve the public good problem.

The core problem is obtaining the knowledge necessary to provide the 'right' amount of the good. Market failures emerge from the inability of unhampered markets to achieve allocative efficiency – in the case of public goods this results in an under-supply of the good. In theory, government interventions can contribute to the achievement of this ideal by increasing production. This justification for government intervention in the market assumes, however, that government agents know the optimal level of output necessary to achieve allocative efficiency. There is no reason to believe that political actors have special access to this information, which as Hayek (1945) pointed out is in fact generated only through the market process in the first place.

Government interventions to increase the production of public goods do not mean that the 'right' amount has been produced. Indeed, while government can produce or subsidise the production of a good, it does not mean that allocative efficiency has been achieved. In the absence of market criteria – prices and profit/loss accounting – for gauging the level of output, government officials will be left to guess the correct level. Even if officials know that a particular good is under-supplied on the market and therefore that more should be produced, there is no reason to think that they will produce the correct amount. In attempting to correct the under-supply they may in fact create an over-supply larger in magnitude than the market under-provision. This is problematic since, from an efficiency standpoint, over-supplying a good, just like under-supplying the good, is inefficient. So while happiness scholars praise how happiness taxes will not only increase happiness but also supply additional public goods, there is reason for scepticism regarding government's ability to deliver these objectives.

A final problem with using happiness taxes to provide public goods is that it is unclear that these goods will increase happiness. Indeed, if people suffer from being on a hedonic treadmill whereby they ultimately return to a baseline of happiness, then surely this must also apply to public goods. This means that even if we assume that policymakers know what public goods to supply, the provision of these goods will lead to only a temporary spike in happiness followed by a return to the original baseline.

If the goal is to increase happiness, increasing public goods is not the way to do it on the very terms put forth by happiness scholars. Finally, those holding the power to decide what public goods to supply and in what quantities hold positions of status which, according to happiness scholars, will make the very citizens they seek to help less happy.

Concluding remarks

We have raised several conceptual and practical issues with happiness economics. In concluding, we would like to provide an alternative means of thinking about issues of happiness and wellbeing. Instead of focusing on designing specific policies and interventions that seek to maximise some notion of happiness, we would like to suggest that focus should instead be placed on the meta-institutions that frame individuals' actions. Given that happiness is subjective in nature and there is no universal definition of happiness, it is our contention that a flourishing human life is one where the individual has the freedom to discover and pursue whatever it is that maximises his or her own wellbeing. For some a flourishing life will be characterised by a workaholic lifestyle; for others it will consist of a life dedicated to philanthropy and charity. According to this view, the institutions necessary for the pursuit of happiness are those that protect individual and economic freedoms.

Hayek argued that market competition is a discovery procedure through which people determine the best way to achieve their ends. Similar logic can be applied to the pursuit of happiness. As Lee writes, 'Achieving happiness is an ongoing project, not something that can be accomplished once and for all ...' He goes on to note that 'The argument that the pursuit of money, which after all is a general claim on a wide range of things, is futile because more money doesn't permanently increase happiness can be generalised to almost all, if not all, pursuits' (Lee, 2005: 394). Instead of attempting to centrally plan and micro-manage happiness, the focus must be on ensuring the existence of institutions associated with social and economic autonomy. Only when these conditions of autonomy are in place will individuals be able to discover and pursue whatever their notion of happiness may entail.

References

Buchanan, J. M. (1969), *Cost and Choice: An Inquiry in Economic Theory*, Chicago, IL: Chicago University Press.

Cowen, T. (2000), *What Price Fame?*, Cambridge, MA: Harvard University Press.

Easterlin, R. A. (1974), 'Does economic growth improve the human lot? Some empirical evidence', in P. A. David and M. W. Reder (eds), *Nations and Households in Economic Growth: Essays in Honor of Moses Abramowitz*, New York: Academic Press, pp. 89–125.

Frank, R. (1999), *Luxury Fever: Money and Happiness in an Era of Excess*, Princeton, NJ: Princeton University Press.

Frey, B. S. and A. Stutzer (2002a), 'What can economists learn from happiness research', *Journal of Economics Literature*, 40(2): 402–35.

Frey, B. S. and A. Stutzer (2002b), *Happiness and Economics: How the Economy and Institutions Affect Human Well-being*, Princeton, NJ: Princeton University Press.

Griffith, T. D. (2004), 'Progressive taxation and happiness', *Boston College Law Review*, 45(5), 1363–98.

Hayek, F. A. (1945), 'The use of knowledge in society', *American Economic Review*, 35(4): 519–30.

Hayek, F. A. (1976), *Law, Legislation and Liberty*, vol. 2: *The Mirage of Social Justice*, Chicago, IL: University of Chicago Press.

Kirzner, I. (1979), 'The perils of regulation: a market-process approach', in *Discovery and the Capitalist Process*, Chicago, IL: Chicago University Press, pp. 119–49.

Kling, A. (2004), 'The happiness police', Tech Central Station, 5 August, http://www.ideasinactiontv.com/tcs_daily/2004/08/the-happiness-police.html, accessed 4 January 2011.

Layard, R. (2005), *Happiness: Lessons from a new science*, New York: Penguin Press.

Lee, D. R. (2005), 'Who says money cannot buy happiness?', *Independent Review*, X(3): 385–400.

Mitchell, W. and R. T. Simmons (2004), *Beyond Politics: Markets, Welfare, and the Failure of Bureaucracy*, Oakland, CA: Independent Institute.

Robbins, L. (1932), *An Essay on the Nature and Significance of Economic Science*, London: Macmillan.

Wilkinson, W. (2007), *In Pursuit of Happiness Research. Is it reliable? What Does it Imply for Policy?*, Cato Institute Policy Analysis no. 590, Washington, DC: Cato Institute.

9 HAPPINESS IS NOT WITHIN THE GOVERNMENT'S REMIT: THE PHILOSOPHICAL FLAW IN HAPPINESS ECONOMICS

Pedro Schwartz

Utilitarianism is the watermark of British social philosophy. Though not always fully explicit it is ever present as a fallback position. One must be thankful to Lord Layard, one of the main champions of happiness economics, for making his kind of Benthamism explicit: a utilitarianism that assumes that the feeling of happiness is a value that trumps all other social goods. As such, I will concentrate my attention on Layard's utilitarianism. A contribution to the critical evaluation of happiness economics is all the more urgent since this viewpoint has become fashionable not only among socialists in search of a mission but also among conservatives in denial of individualism. I will try to show that Layard's fundamental utilitarianism has three unwelcome consequences: first, that by elevating happiness to the rank of the supreme value of social life he commits the naturalistic fallacy and thus unduly narrows the field of normative economics; secondly, that by making happiness a public good he unnecessarily invades civil liberties and joins those who fail to distinguish between negative freedom and positive freedom; and thirdly, that he conflates the morality of personal relations within small groups with the ethics of the Open Society, when in large societies progress demands competition rather than contentment. The conclusion is that a happy society should not be an aim of public policy.

Layard's utilitarianism

In the third of his Robbins Memorial Lectures (2003), Layard defends the need for a comprehensive moral theory to guide us in everyday life and in situations of moral difficulty. He points out something that is true, namely that today 'there are no agreed concepts of how unselfish a person should be or of what constitutes a good society'; but he assumes that the good society needs a unifying moral theory, something which is arguable, to say the least. He notes that present-day philosophers offer no overarching theory that would help us to resolve all our moral dilemmas. Instead, he says, they support various separate values: 'promise-keeping, kindness, truthfulness, fairness and so on'. To fill the need for a unifying principle of personal and social morality he proposes Bentham's classical utilitarianism. As he says: 'I want to suggest that the right concept is the old Enlightenment one of the greatest happiness. The good society is the one where people are happiest. And the right action is the one which produces the greatest happiness' (ibid.).

Lord Layard thus bases his happiness economics on a Benthamite foundation: in our societies we should not value productive efficiency or economic growth or individual liberty in themselves but should seek to maximise the overall amount of happiness.[1] The negative externalities of rivalrous behaviour and

---

1   Layard seems to be unaware in his *Robbins Lectures* (2003) of the fact that utilitarianism at the present time has come in for heavy criticism by many authors who are as keen as he is for government to display active public policies in the promotion of the good society. He only mentions Sen's strictures on mere addition of individual happiness in Lecture III, when Sen's capability approach (1999) goes far beyond classical utilitarianism, to say nothing of Rawls's demand that in the good society a minimum of the all-purpose means (including income and wealth) that individuals need to pursue their interests and to maintain their self-respect as free and equal persons should be supplied (1999).

workaholism that Layard sees as a cause of the under-supply of happiness in advanced economies are surely not large enough to justify the use of taxation to dampen excessive growth and discourage conspicuous consumption.

Layard's brand of happiness economics raises three fundamental questions:

- Is it possible to organise society around a single overriding goal, such as maximising observable happiness?
- Is the tendency of the free market to promote excessive rivalry and foster conspicuous consumption a 'public bad' to be corrected by taxes or subsidies?
- Should benevolence, the expression of a morality of happiness in personal relations, also be the ethical rule in market transactions?

As an indication of my reasons to answer *No* to all three questions I will first say that Layard should not have deplored the absence of general agreement on an overarching principle to define the good society. One of the theses of this chapter is precisely that in a free society there cannot and should not be a single defined goal to guide our social life.

On the second question, whether happiness is a public good, we know after reading Coase on lighthouses that there are no *pure* public goods. All goods have a private dimension and the public element of most can often be safely ignored when their supply by private means is ample (Coase, 1975). The idea that government is able to foster social happiness by reining in the human tendency to compete and emulate by means of taxes and subsidies seems to be a case of bad 'partial equilibrium' economics. It also opens the door to an undue invasion of civil liberties.

Thirdly, the benevolent wish to make people happy should not be the guiding principle of both personal morality and social ethics. This is not to say that politics is beyond morality, as Machiavelli famously proposed, but that personal morality and social ethics cannot be of the same nature. The rules that govern relations among persons who know each other will be different from those that pertain to anonymous transactions in a great society: personal benevolence in the one case, abstract justice in the other. Benevolence is indeed the principal virtue when relating with family, friends, associates and partners. It is misplaced, however, as the supreme ethical principle of society as a whole. To propose this single principle to guide us in all our dealings, personal and societal, is to overlook the inevitable conflict in progressive societies between the rules of benevolence that should guide us in our conduct towards our neighbour and the abstract rules of justice we must obey in what Hayek called the Great Society.

An overriding aim for public policy?

Utilitarianism and the naturalistic fallacy

For Jeremy Bentham happiness or utility was not a formal concept but had material content. He started the *Introduction to the Principles of Morals and Legislation* (1970 [1789]) with the following bold words: 'Nature has placed mankind under the governance of two sovereign masters, *pain* and *pleasure*. It is for them alone to point out what we ought to do, as well as to determine what we shall do. On the one hand the standard of right and wrong, on the other the chain of causes and effects, are fastened to their throne.'

The first doubt posed by these words, indeed by the very title of Bentham's essay, is the implied pole-vault from natural inclinations to moral obligation. If men necessarily act at the behest of nature, as prompted by their feelings of pain and pleasure, what is the point of writing pages and pages to tell them what their duties are? Preaching would seem to be unnecessary if men obey their sovereign masters, come what may. If, on the other hand, the interests of individual men and women are not in natural harmony, why should it be the duty of anybody to refrain from uncooperative behaviour or stop others from so behaving? Public-spirited utilitarianism would, at first sight, be a contradiction in terms.

All would be well if the spontaneous working of the market naturally brought about a harmony of interests. But Bentham did not believe the market would of itself bring about this harmony.[2] Public intervention was indispensable. Hence he was led to frame a rule to divide good public policy from bad. 'The interest of the community then is, what? – the sum of the interests of the several members who compose it.'

Bentham chose summing over individuals each counting for one, for he discounted the greater sensitivity of different individuals to pain or pleasure. Hence: '[a] measure of government (which is but a particular kind of action, performed by a particular person or persons) may be said to be conformable to or dictated by the principle of utility, when ... the tendency which it has to augment the happiness of the community is

2   'I have not, I never had, nor ever shall have, any horror, sentimental or anarchical, of the hand of government. I leave it to Adam Smith, and the champions of the rights of man ... to talk of invasions of natural liberty, and to give as a special argument against this or that law, an argument the effect of which would be to put a negative upon all laws' (Bentham, 1954: 257–8).

greater than any which it has to diminish it'.[3]

This really was no help in answering the question: why *should* anyone sacrifice her or his interest for the sake of the common weal? Why indeed should people in power care for the interest of the public rather than their own? Why should the losers in the social welfare calculus be reconciled to the need to attain social harmony at their cost? There could only be one answer – to wit, that on the basis of rational long-term calculation such a sacrifice of short-term interests could be shown to be for the good of all. But this would have to be on condition that other people would also be rational in this manner – or be made to behave rationally. An enlightened despot was needed to enforce 'rational' behaviour on recalcitrants or, if there was no despot of this kind, a body of citizens organised by a democratic constitution.[4]

The point here is that the general acquiescence to the rule of an enlightened utilitarian despot or the agreement on a utilitarian constitution implies that a society can be organised around the single overarching principle of the maximisation of the sum of happiness. The logical difficulty of moving from *is* to *ought* disappears when there are no 'oughts' to choose from, only one

---

3 By this, of course, he meant the sum of pleasure or happiness net of pain. There could be other public rules starting from the same pain–pleasure psychology of individuals, such as Rawls's second principle of Justice which favours the poor.

4 Bentham's first efforts were indeed directed at convincing the powerful, e.g. Catherine of Russia. It was only around 1809, when he was in his sixties, that Bentham began to see that as a *practical* theory his utilitarianism was incomplete unless embedded in radical democracy. He thus started a fruitful line of research that culminated in his unfinished *Constitutional Code* (1830). He there drew up interesting institutional devices to align the interests of governors and governed, a clear anticipation of public choice theory and the law and economics movement: Dinwiddy (2003 [1975]).

– namely, the maximisation of happiness. Public ethics is then reduced to a problem of operations research.

Logical reasons that forbid moving from 'is' statements to 'ought' statements elicit strong resistance among many political economists. They want economic policy to be 'scientific' to be sure of its rationality. But rather than rehearse Hume's argument (1739), I will point out one of the dangers of uncritically inducing values from facts: too much confidence in what facts seem to tell us blinds us to the possibility of alternative moral prescriptions.

This is the case in Layard's factual arguments for utilitarian ethics. Layard adduces evidence from neuroscience to conclude that utility can be measured cardinally and compared interpersonally. That is as may be but it is no reason for making utilitarianism the ultimate moral criterion in society. Thus, Layard recounts a number of neurological experiments where reactions of different people to pleasurable and painful stimuli can be shown to be constant for each person and similar among persons.[5] The correlation between stimulus and reaction in these experiments, he says, first:

> ... applies quite accurately over time within each individual, providing a solid basis for the notion that happiness is a cardinal variable, rising and falling just like your blood pressure. And, second, the correlation holds strongly across people, confirming our view that happiness can be compared between people. (Layard, 2003: Lecture I)

---

5   Reactions to pleasure on the left side of the brain and to pain on the right side (for right-handed people) can be tracked with the help of functional magnetic resonance imaging. On being shown agreeable and disagreeable pictures the reactions of different people can be shown to be constant and similar (Layard, 2003: Lecture I, where Layard summarises the work of Richard Davidson at Wisconsin University).

After positing the cardinality of utility for each of us and the possibility of interpersonal comparisons of happiness, Layard says that this affords a solid basis for successfully devising public policies to try to make everyone happier. But why should the greatest happiness of the greatest number be the principal rule for our personal life and for society?

People are in fact moved by values other than happiness and are often confronted by clashes between values that all claim to be basic. If Antigone had only been a superstitious young woman and Creon a cruel self-seeking tyrant the play would become banal drama. Two basic values are in conflict, sisterly piety and the weight of the purple. What lifts the conflict to a higher plane is that both characters wish to do what is right. There would be no tragedy if characters were simply trying to be happy and perhaps make others happy.[6] Socrates took hemlock, not because he looked forward to an eternity in the Elysian Fields but because the god commanded him to seek truth and virtue. Galileo would have been better advised not to insist that sceptical princes of the Church peer at the moons of Jupiter through his new glass. He did not do so to be happy or make them happy but to show them the Truth.

A single overarching principle masks ethical dilemmas

It is of the essence of free societies that they are not organised

---

6   Creon in Sophocles's original tragedy is an erratic autocrat (Hall, 2010). My remarks are inspired by Anouilh's *Antigone* (2008 [1944]), where Creon is no consistently inconsistent character but a politician intent on saving the state. The modern Antigone rejects Creon's call to understand his motives and marry Hemon and be happy: 'I am not here to understand. I am here to say No and to die.'

for the pursuit of a single goal, not even the goal of freedom. As explained below, civil liberty cannot be seen as a substantive or material goal since it consists of the absence of undue coercion. It is a negative principle, in that it does not prescribe but forbids and protects. Civil liberty is a framework within which individuals, singly or in association with others, choose their ends without undue or illegal interference. Its essence is private property, tort and contract law.

It is only at the time of war, especially total war, that societies can be said to have a single overriding goal. Lionel Robbins, speaking immediately after the end of World War II (Robbins, 1947: Lecture II), was especially perceptive in the discussion of the change that comes over a free society when it is forced to wage total war. When the alternative is death or victory, said Robbins, the economic problem is drastically simplified: 'In total war there is only one prime object of policy, the achievement of total victory.' Free market decisions are replaced by price fixing and rationing, on the one hand, and an all-embracing control of supplies, including conscription, on the other. A special problem for Robbins was why the controls that were put in the place of the market 'succeeded as well as they did'. His answer to this conundrum was that control from the centre worked in war because of the part played 'by the sense of social obligation and unity of purpose which our perils invoked'. The crucial words in that sentence are 'unity of purpose', one of whose symptoms was 'the comparative infrequency of black market activities'.

Once the war is over, however, 'you can no longer express the object of economic policy in terms of a single concrete objective'. The yearning for national unity is always present but then communally inclined economists are reduced to giving 'a formal description of the ultimate goal which has a unitary appearance'. This is what they do when they say 'that the object of policy should be to maximise welfare over time', though this is simply 'to state the problem, not to solve it'. The reason is that in times of peace the problem becomes one of allocation, not of priority, as in war. Once the single end is replaced by a variety of aims, there is 'no objective measure either of the conflicting ends or the effectiveness of alternative means'. Any imposed apportionment of priority among ends becomes arbitrary. The question is not solved by voting: 'the more democratic you try to be, the more difficult the task becomes'.

The first two critical remarks on Layard's happiness economics are therefore the following. First, inducing a normative rule from factual observations – for example, about pleasure and pain – tends to hide the influence of other norms on human behaviour. Secondly, that proposing a single overarching norm to govern social ethics makes society ungovernable except in times of war, when the aim of survival appears to overcome every other norm.

Happiness as a public good

Rivalrous labour as a public bad

For Layard, the rivalry of individuals 'to keep up with the Joneses' leads them to work far too much for their own good or for the good of their family and their community. People do not compete for show in the amount of leisure they enjoy. Leisure is simply valued for itself. But it is otherwise with income. Individuals exert themselves to increase their income not only for its own sake but also to be able to engage in conspicuous consumption. They work harder than is really needed so as to keep their relative position in society. Seen from the point of view of happiness, they consume less leisure than they would prefer if the rivalry with their equals did not 'force' them, so to speak, to exert themselves too much. They would not mind working a little less as long as others did the same. It does not matter for the sake of the argument whether one calls this reaction envy or rivalry. Its indirect or external effects are harmful both to the individual and to society.

Based on fieldwork results, Layard asserts that 'if my income increases, the loss of happiness to everybody else is about 30% of the gain in happiness to me'. Now comes the crucial assertion: 'This is a form of pollution, and to discourage excessive pollution, the polluter should pay for the disbenefit he causes.' The conclusion is a public policy recommendation: 'So the polluter should lose 30 pence out of every 100 pence that he earns – a tax rate of 30% on all additional income. Assuming the tax proceeds are returned to him through useful public spending, he will work less hard – and the self-defeating element in work will have been eliminated.'

Leisure a 'public good'

The public good argument made by Layard suffers from the fact that he has effectively ignored all the work on the economics of externalities since Pigou. It is possible, in theory, that leisure might be a public good in the way he describes – though I am sceptical. But all goods, to some degree, provide externalities, and the state cannot and should not undertake the calculations to try to determine the 'optimal' production of each. Furthermore, public choice economics tells us that the state apparatus that is set up to deal with this problem will, itself, be subject to externalities and other imperfections. There has to be an overwhelming case for intervention to produce a public good.

Coase's paper 'Lighthouse economics' (1975) showed how the great majority of the lighthouses of Great Britain up to 1830 had been built by private enterprise and how their owners were able to make a great deal of money when these facilities were purchased by the public. The famous Samuelson textbook *Economics* had presented lighthouses as a typical case of public goods, whose supply could not match their social usefulness because the ships using them could not be charged for it on the high seas. Coase discovered that ships repairing to British ports were charged by port officials on the evidence of their log books for using light-houses on their way to harbour. Of course, ships that bypassed the British Isles continued their voyage scot-free, but this deficiency could be overlooked if enough traffic entered port. The important lesson from this is that all goods have a public dimension. Only in the case of the few whose 'publicness', so to speak, is so large must they be mainly financed with taxes. To say the least, this is highly questionable in the case of the apparent public goods that Layard identifies.

Indeed, it is highly questionable in the case of happiness economics that the negative externality of hard work and conspic-uous consumption is large that the state must intervene; there are also external beneficial effects from hard work and enterprise. Layard recognises this by suggesting that his ideas would not be appropriate in underdeveloped countries. Furthermore, the situa-tion differs between individuals. How are we to know whether the good effects of hard work outweigh the bad effects and to what extent in different circumstances? An unmarried individual may wish to work fifteen hours a day because his work and his social life are synonymous; when the same person is married with a family, the trade-offs – and external effects – will be different. A uniform tax rate treats all people as if they are identical and with preferences as if they are known by the utilitarian central planner.

From Coase's lighthouse story, we also know that public goods can be provided by the market to a much greater extent than economists had often realised before his work. In terms of the work/leisure trade-off, local conventions and holidays, decisions about business closure and holidays taken by large employers and so on all help to socialise the leisure decision without central planning. The idea that the monitoring of brain signals can be used to develop an optimal tax on work for all individuals so as to produce the greatest happiness for the greatest number is a typical conceit of central planning.

Happiness economics and civil liberty

One of the conclusions of Layard's analysis is that personal taxation in countries that have reached a plateau of happiness must be high, especially at the margin:

> So what is the appropriate level of taxation at the margin?
> The quantitative evidence is only beginning to accumulate,
> but I have already suggested 30 per cent to deal with
> rivalry, and the evidence suggests at least as much to
> deal with habituation. Thus 60 per cent would not seem
> inappropriate, and that is in fact the typical level of
> marginal taxation in Europe – if you allow for direct and
> indirect taxes. (Layard, 2003: Lecture I)

This has obvious consequences for personal freedom. Layard is reconciled to this effect because his doctrine of civil liberty is of the kind Isaiah Berlin called 'positive' and I prefer to call 'possessive'.

It has become fashionable to discount Isaiah Berlin's distinction between negative and positive freedom. His concept of freedom either is declared too narrow or the distinction itself rejected because negative freedom is subsumed under positive. For Layard, however, freedom is a more fuzzy concept: 'There are at least three dimensions to freedom [he says]: political influence (on government policy); personal freedom (e.g. free speech); and economic freedom (to do business)' (ibid.: Lecture III, p. 9). Amartya Sen, for his part, in *Development as Freedom* (1999), mentions five distinct freedoms: political freedoms, economic facilities, social opportunities, transparency guarantees and protective security. But, as Berlin put it with his inimitable good sense, 'liberty is liberty, not equality or fairness or justice or culture, or human happiness or a quiet conscience' (1969 [1958]: 125).

I rather dislike the term 'negative' for the concept of *liberty from* the unlawful interference of others in my life and property. And calling 'positive' the view that one is not free unless one has the means to enjoy *liberty for* doing as one wishes makes so-called positive freedom sound much more attractive than it deserves.

Classical or formal liberty is not negative, except in that it consists of the possibility to say 'No' to undue invasions of our personal sphere. For Berlin, personal liberty meant not suffering violence or coercion. It had to be distinguished from the possession of means, opportunities or, as Sen calls them, 'functionings'[7]

---

7   Sen (1992: 40). A person's functionings 'can vary from such elementary things as being adequately nourished, being in good health, ... to more complex

that allow one to unfold one's personality or achieve one's happiness or belong to a respected group. Unfortunately, the fostering of possessive liberty often comes at the expense of formal liberty. We know from experience that the welfare state with its various entitlements undermines the personal responsibility needed for the self-government of free men. I need only quote Sen on 'indirect liberty' to make my point: 'What a person would have chosen if he actually had control is an important consideration in judging the person's liberty. ... The social-choice characterization of liberty compares what emerges with what a person *would have chosen* (though not necessarily chosen by him).' Arrant paternalism.

I want to underline the importance of formal liberties precisely for the very poor. What seems to be a protection only for the rich is an essential defence for the poor, the concubine and the pariah. Without habeas corpus, minimal property rights, respect for the agreements reached with the employer, the husband, the landlord, without the right to vote, the 'prole' cannot even set foot on the path towards greater wellbeing for him or his family. High taxation for the 'rich' soon becomes high taxes for the middle class and the poor: taxes introduced for the happiness of society soon become high wasteful expenditure for all.

My conclusion is that the happiness economics that Lord Layard has built on utilitarian foundations elevates envy to the category of a public virtue, endangers political liberty and shackles social progress.

---

achievements such as being happy, having self-respect, taking part in the life of the community ... [T]he capability to achieve functionings ... constitute[s] the person's freedom – the real opportunities – to have well-being ... "well-being freedom"'.

The justice of the market

The tribe and the market

We now move on to the central questions. Does civilisation make us happy? Is happiness a good guide for the progress of our societies? In Chapter 10 of the first volume of *The Open Society and Its Enemies* Popper came face to face with the need to understand why Platonic political philosophy has been so successful down the ages. After a long search he was forced to the conclusion that 'both the old and the new totalitarian movements rested on the fact that they attempted to answer a very real need': '[I]t appears to me that Plato's declaration to make the state and its citizens happy is not mere propaganda. I am ready to grant his fundamental benevolence. I also grant that he was right, to a limited extent, in the sociological analysis on which he based his promise of happiness.'

When reporting these thoughts of Popper's one needs to add that, of course, not all philosophers who hanker after a happy society are totalitarians. It is true, however, that they usually feel some hostility towards commerce and competition, the founts of the Open Society, because they make many in the population unhappy. To proceed with Popper's analysis of the Abstract Society: '... Plato, with deep sociological insight, found that his contemporaries were suffering under a severe strain, and that this strain was due to the social revolution which had begun with the rise of democracy and individualism' (1957 [1945]: 171–2).

Life in the tribe accords better with our inherited traits. When society moves away from functioning like an organism the result can be unsettling.

> [A]n open society may become by degrees, what I should like to term an 'abstract society'. We could conceive of a society in which men practically never meet face to face – in which all business is conducted by individuals in isolation who communicate by typed letters or by telegrams, and who go about in closed motorcars ... Of course, there never will be or can be a completely abstract or predominantly abstract society.

As Popper concluded: '[A]lthough society has become abstract, the biological make-up of man has not changed much; men have social needs which they cannot satisfy in an abstract society' (ibid.: 174–5).

The opaque character of the Great Society

These thoughts of Popper's as relayed by Hayek when speaking of the Great Society give us an inkling of why there is such resistance to the market economy and globalisation in advanced countries, though perhaps not so much in successful emerging economies. Firstly, the kind of society in which we now live is difficult to understand and therefore to accept. Social institutions are not visible except in a symbolic form and can only be described with the help of approximate mental models. Thus, the economic market has only observable, partial manifestations but cannot be grasped in its entirety. Equally, money is used by everyone but not perceived in all its ramifications.

Secondly, the perception of the structure and functions of social institutions is made more difficult because they are neither natural nor rational. As Hayek noted in the 'Epilogue' to volume III of his *Law, Legislation and Liberty* (1982 [1979]): '[t]he basic tools of civilization – language, morals, law and money – are all the result of spontaneous growth and not of design, and of the last two organized power has got hold and thoroughly corrupted them' (ibid.: 163).

Thirdly, the customs and rules of the market economy clash with much of our inherited make-up and perhaps make us 'unhappy'. There are many features of an open society that go against the grain of our nature as it was formed during the many centuries of tribal life, and Hayek gives a number of examples of 'unnatural' practices prevalent in market economies: 'the toleration of bartering with the outsider, the recognition of delimited private property, especially in land, the enforcement of contractual obligations, the competition with fellow craftsmen in the same trade, the variability of initially customary prices, the lending of money, particularly at interest ...' (ibid.: 161).

These practices grate with the customs of small face-to-face societies where our instinctive moral reactions were formed.

The harsh discipline of freedom

All this leads Hayek to underline that the rules and institutions of the Great Society that are essential for our progress and freedom do not have the backing of the natural or the rational. To start with, '[t]he morals which maintain the open society do not serve to gratify human emotions'. Since the open society was never an aim of evolution (if evolution can have an aim), the emotions imprinted in the human breast only told man 'what he ought to do in the kind of society in which he had lived in the dim past'. In fact, the rules learnt by cultural selection '... became necessary chiefly in order to repress some of the innate rules which were adapted to the hunting and gathering life of the small bands of fifteen to forty persons, led by a headman and defending a territory against all outsiders' (ibid.: 161–2).

Neither have the ethics of the Great Society been devised by our reason. As Adam Ferguson pointed out 250 years ago, echoed, of course, by von Mises in the last century, our institutions are the result of human action but not of human design.

This disharmony in civilised life makes it impossible to use happiness as a guide for all the decisions that we must make in today's societies. The natural impulses of pleasure and pain are not the guide we need in a commercial society. Utilitarianism is basically flawed because it tries to base the ethics of the Open Society on the natural impulses of pain and pleasure. Again, as Hayek points out, pleasure is not the end we have strived for in evolution but simply a signal that led individuals to do what was usually required for the preservation of the group. In sum: *'man has been civilized very much against his wishes'* (ibid.: 168, emphasis in original). Constructivist utilitarian theories derive their rules from a desire to serve individual pleasure as an end in itself. There is no guarantee that the application of such theories will allow the Great Society to survive. The Great Society has not come about as a result of consciously trying to promote the maximisation of happiness and it cannot be assumed that it will survive if we consciously pursue that aim.

We can see how the deliberate attempt to create a society based on utilitarian calculation of pain, pleasure and happiness will undermine the Great Society by proposing particular policy options. Especially cruel punishments, very strict immigration policies, restrictions on trade and so on are all policies that could well raise measured happiness. The desire to punish, the fear of people unknown to us and the desire to protect our own businesses are natural instincts that may well be – or may well have been – important for the survival of the small group. They are, however, inimical to the maintenance of the Great Society upon which our civilisation and prosperity (and long-run welfare) rest. They are therefore not a good guide to public policy even if individuals or small groups acting freely may wish to adopt some of those principles in their everyday life.

The moral rejection of the market economy

The instinctive rejection of the ethics of the open society has an unexpected effect: it leads ordinary people to fret about the conclusions of economics even when they are well established and tested. This makes the life of the classical economist a frustrating experience. Our science of economics seems to oppose the fond beliefs and moral principles of ordinary people, so that markets go unloved and suffer continual interference.

In a recent clear-sighted essay, Clark and Lee (2011) underline the fact that the conclusions of economic analysis are often rejected out of hand because of the ethics seen to sustain it. The political economy of the market, whether right or wrong in its factual conclusions and predictions, is felt to be downright immoral by many. It is said to be based on greed, to be devoid of human feelings, even to undermine the very morality of hard work and self-disciplined calculation that made its success. These misguided beliefs are nourished by the clash between ordinary morality and the impersonal ethics of the market.

The clash of two moralities in progressive societies must be acknowledged if the market is to be freed from the kind of interference implicit in happiness economics. Clark and Lee separate themselves clearly from utilitarianism as a generally acceptable rule of morality and proceed to distinguish between two types of duty-based morality: 'magnanimous morality' and 'mundane morality':

> Magnanimous morality can best be defined in terms of helping others in ways that satisfy three characteristics – helping intentionally, doing so at a personal sacrifice, and providing the help to identifiable beneficiaries ... Mundane morality can be described broadly as obeying the generally accepted rules or norms of conduct such as telling the truth, honouring your promises and contractual obligations, respecting the property rights of others, and refraining from intentionally harming others. (Ibid.: 3, 6)

Beneficence, Adam Smith said, referring to what Clark and Lee call magnanimous morality: '... is less essential to the existence of society than justice ... Beneficence ... is the ornament which embellishes, not the foundation which supports the building ... Justice or mundane morality, on the contrary, is the main pillar that upholds the whole edifice' (1976 [1759]: 86).

Mundane morality, while being essential for the existence of society, is much less attractive to ordinary people and in fact often not recognised as morality at all. This is because, contrary to magnanimous morality, mundane morality has three characteristics that contrast with the three set out above: it is self-interested, profitable – for both sides – and dispersed among anonymous transactors. That is why, say the authors, Smith's 'invisible hand' is so little regarded in ordinary discourse.

Now we can see why mundane morality is seen in such an unfavourable light by people who do not recognise that it has much more general and beneficent effects in society than personal magnanimity. Thus, it shocks people to hear that Bill Gates or Warren Buffet have done much more good in business than with their charitable endeavours. In sum: 'it is much easier to understand the persistent criticism of markets, and of the invisible hand justification for them, once the strong emotional attachment to magnanimous morality is considered' (Clark and Lee, 2011: 7–8).

The inevitable moral conflict at the heart of a free society

I will conclude this philosophical criticism of happiness economics with a warning against the mistake of applying magnanimous moral rules to the functioning of the economic market. An ethical monism based on natural morality creates confusion in the judgement of well-meaning people about the character of transactions in the economic market, where 'non-tuism' mostly rules, thus endangering liberty and interfering with capitalist progress. Conversely, ethical monism is not permissible when trying to apply free market ethics to personal intercourse. Clark and Lee aptly quote Hayek (1988: 18) on this point:

> If we were to apply the unmodified, uncurbed, rules of the micro-cosmos (i.e., of the small band or troop, or of say, our families) to the macro-cosmos (our wider civilization), as our instincts and sentimental yearnings, often make us wish to do, *we would destroy it*. Yet, if we were always to apply the rules of the extended order to our more intimate groupings, *we would crush them*. So we must learn to live in two sorts of worlds at once.

Happiness economics, which tries to extend a deficient hedonic morality to the arrangements of an open society, must be pronounced an unworkable project.

References

Anouilh, J. (2008 [1944]), *Antigone*, Paris: La Table Ronde.

Bentham, J. (1830), *Constitutional Code*, in *The Collected Works of Jeremy Bentham*, vol. I, ed. F. Rosen and J. H. Burns, Oxford: Clarendon Press.

Bentham, J. (1954), 'Defence of a maximum', in *Economic Writings*, vol. III, ed. W. Stark, London: Royal Economic Society, pp. 257–8.

Bentham, J. (1970 [1789]), *An Introduction to the Principles of Morals and Legislation* (MS 1780, 1st edn 1789, 2nd edn 1823), ed. J. H. Burns and H. A. L. Hart for *The Collected Works of Jeremy Bentham*, London: University of London and the Athlone Press.

Berlin, I. (1969 [1958]), 'Two concepts of liberty', in *Four Essays on Liberty*, Oxford: Oxford University Press.

Clark, J. R. and D. R. Lee (2011), 'Markets and morality', *Cato Journal*, 31(1): 1–25.

Coase, R. (1975), 'Lighthouse economics', *Journal of Law and Economics*, 17(2): 357–76.

Dinwiddy, J. (2003 [1975]), 'Bentham's transition to political radicalism', in W. Twining (ed.), *Bentham: The Selected Writings of John Dinwiddy*, Stanford, CA: Stanford University Press.

Ferguson, A. (1967 [1767]), *An Essay on the History of Civil Society*. Extracts published in *The Scottish Moralists on Human Nature and Society*, ed. L. Schneider, Chicago, IL: University of Chicago Press.

Hall, E. (2010), *Greek Tragedy. Suffering under the Sun*, Oxford: Oxford University Press.

Hayek, F. A. (1982 [1979]), 'Epilogue: the three sources of human values', in *Law, Legislation and Liberty. A new statement of the liberal principles of justice and political economy*, vol. III: *The Political Order of a Free People*, London: Routledge & Kegan Paul.

Hayek, F. A. (1988), *The Fatal Conceit. The Errors of Socialism*, Chicago, IL, and London: University of Chicago Press and Routledge.

Hume, D. (1739), *A Treatise of Human Nature*, many edns.

Layard, R. (2003), *Lionel Robbins Memorial Lectures 2002/3*, I: 'Happiness: has social science a clue?'; II: 'Income and happiness: re-thinking economic policy'; III: 'What would make a happier society', London School of Economics, 3, 4 and 5 March.

Popper, K. R. (1957 [1945]), *The Open Society and Its Enemies*, 3rd revised edn, London: Routledge & Kegan Paul.

Rawls, J. (1999), *A Theory of Justice*, revised edn, Cambridge, MA: Harvard University Press.

Robbins, L. (1947), *The Economic Problem in Peace and War. Some Reflections on Objectives and Mechanisms*, London School of Economics.

Sen, A. K. (1983), 'Liberty and social choice', *Journal of Philosophy*, 80(1): 5–28.

Sen, A. K. (1992), *Inequality Reexamined*, Oxford: Clarendon Press.

Sen, A. K. (1999), *Development as Freedom*, Oxford: Oxford University Press.

Smith, Adam (1976 [1759]), *The Theory of Moral Sentiments*, ed. D. D. Raphael and A. L. MacFie, Oxford: Clarendon Press.

ABOUT THE IEA

The Institute is a research and educational charity (No. CC 235 351), limited by guarantee. Its mission is to improve understanding of the fundamental institutions of a free society by analysing and expounding the role of markets in solving economic and social problems.

The IEA achieves its mission by:

- a high-quality publishing programme
- conferences, seminars, lectures and other events
- outreach to school and college students
- brokering media introductions and appearances

The IEA, which was established in 1955 by the late Sir Antony Fisher, is an educational charity, not a political organisation. It is independent of any political party or group and does not carry on activities intended to affect support for any political party or candidate in any election or referendum, or at any other time. It is financed by sales of publications, conference fees and voluntary donations.

In addition to its main series of publications the IEA also publishes a termly journal, *Economic Affairs*.

The IEA is aided in its work by a distinguished international Academic Advisory Council and an eminent panel of Honorary Fellows. Together with other academics, they review prospective IEA publications, their comments being passed on anonymously to authors. All IEA papers are therefore subject to the same rigorous independent refereeing process as used by leading academic journals.

IEA publications enjoy widespread classroom use and course adoptions in schools and universities. They are also sold throughout the world and often translated/reprinted.

Since 1974 the IEA has helped to create a worldwide network of 100 similar institutions in over 70 countries. They are all independent but share the IEA's mission.

Views expressed in the IEA's publications are those of the authors, not those of the Institute (which has no corporate view), its Managing Trustees, Academic Advisory Council members or senior staff.

Members of the Institute's Academic Advisory Council, Honorary Fellows, Trustees and Staff are listed on the following page.

The Institute gratefully acknowledges financial support for its publications programme and other work from a generous benefaction by the late Alec and Beryl Warren.

247

Other papers recently published by the IEA include:

The Legal Foundations of Free Markets
Edited by Stephen F. Copp
Hobart Paperback 36; ISBN 978 0 255 36591 8; £15.00

Climate Change Policy: Challenging the Activists
Edited by Colin Robinson
Readings 62; ISBN 978 0 255 36595 6; £10.00

Should We Mind the Gap?
Gender Pay Differentials and Public Policy
J. R. Shackleton
Hobart Paper 164; ISBN 978 0 255 36604 5; £10.00

Pension Provision: Government Failure Around the World
Edited by Philip Booth et al.
Readings 63; ISBN 978 0 255 36602 1; £15.00

New Europe's Old Regions
Piotr Zientara
Hobart Paper 165; ISBN 978 0 255 36617 5; £12.50

Central Banking in a Free Society
Tim Congdon
Hobart Paper 166; ISBN 978 0 255 36623 6; £12.50

Verdict on the Crash: Causes and Policy Implications
Edited by Philip Booth
Hobart Paperback 37; ISBN 978 0 255 36635 9; £12.50

The European Institutions as an Interest Group
The Dynamics of Ever-Closer Union
Roland Vaubel
Hobart Paper 167; ISBN 978 0 255 36634 2; £10.00

An Adult Approach to Education
Alison Wolf
Hobart Paper 168; ISBN 978 0 255 36586 4; £10.00

Taxation and Red Tape
The Cost to British Business of Complying with the UK Tax System
Francis Chittenden, Hilary Foster & Brian Sloan
Research Monograph 64; ISBN 978 0 255 36612 0; £12.50

Ludwig von Mises – A Primer
Eamonn Butler
Occasional Paper 143; ISBN 978 0 255 36629 8; £7.50

Does Britain Need a Financial Regulator?
Statutory Regulation, Private Regulation and Financial Markets
Terry Arthur & Philip Booth
Hobart Paper 169; ISBN 978 0 255 36593 2; £12.50

Hayek's *The Constitution of Liberty*
An Account of Its Argument
Eugene F. Miller
Occasional Paper 144; ISBN 978 0 255 36637 3; £12.50

Fair Trade Without the Froth
A Dispassionate Economic Analysis of 'Fair Trade'
Sushil Mohan
Hobart Paper 170; ISBN 978 0 255 36645 8; £10.00

A New Understanding of Poverty
Poverty Measurement and Policy Implications
Kristian Niemietz
Research Monograph 65; ISBN 978 0 255 36638 0; £12.50

The Challenge of Immigration
A Radical Solution
Gary S. Becker
Occasional Paper 145; ISBN 978 0 255 36613 7; £7.50

Sharper Axes, Lower Taxes
Big Steps to a Smaller State
Edited by Philip Booth
Hobart Paperback 38; ISBN 978 0 255 36648 9; £12.50

Self-employment, Small Firms and Enterprise
Peter Urwin
Research Monograph 66; ISBN 978 0 255 36610 6; £12.50

Crises of Governments
The Ongoing Global Financial Crisis and Recession
Robert Barro
Occasional Paper 146; ISBN 978 0 255 36657 1; £7.50

Other IEA publications

Comprehensive information on other publications and the wider work of the IEA can be found at www.iea.org.uk. To order any publication please see below.

Personal customers

Orders from personal customers should be directed to the IEA:
Clare Rusbridge
IEA
2 Lord North Street
FREEPOST LON10168
London SW1P 3YZ
Tel: 020 7799 8907. Fax: 020 7799 2137
Email: crusbridge@iea.org.uk

Trade customers

All orders from the book trade should be directed to the IEA's distributor:
Gazelle Book Services Ltd (IEA Orders)
FREEPOST RLYS-EAHU-YSCZ
White Cross Mills
Hightown
Lancaster LA1 4XS
Tel: 01524 68765. Fax: 01524 53232
Email: sales@gazellebooks.co.uk

IEA subscriptions

The IEA also offers a subscription service to its publications. For a single annual payment (currently £42.00 in the UK), subscribers receive every monograph the IEA publishes. For more information please contact:
Clare Rusbridge
Subscriptions
IEA
2 Lord North Street
FREEPOST LON10168
London SW1P 3YZ
Tel: 020 7799 8907. Fax: 020 7799 2137
Email: crusbridge@iea.org.uk